As a believer, when you're involved in a situation that has you perplexed, worried, or frustrated, you want God's guidance in a hurry. You know that the Bible has the solution you need, but where is it located?

In Bible Answers for King's Kids, Harold Hill gives you biblical references for a myriad of problems that you may face. These readily available solutions assure you that God's loving intervention is continuous. As a King's kid, you'll appreciate Harold Hill's pep talks and insights. And, most importantly, you'll immediately feel God's peace and comfort encompass you as you find the guidance you need in His Word.

Other books by Harold Hill:

How to Live Like a King's Kid
How Did It All Begin? (From Goo to You by Way of
  the Zoo)
How to Be a Winner
How to Live in High Victory
How to Flip Your Flab—Forever
How to Live the Bible Like a King's Kid
God's in Charge Here

If you don't have enough time for all the Bible
reading you need to do, neither do I. That's why
everywhere I go, I listen to Bible tapes on a little cas-
sette player. For ordering information about my favorite version, as well as about the books and teaching
tapes that will help you with attitude control for
victorious living, send a self-addressed, stamped
envelope to:

Harold E. Hill
King's Kids' Korner
P.O. Box 8655
Baltimore, MD 21240
Phone (301) 636-4518

Harold Hill

BIBLE ANSWERS
for
KING'S KIDS

Compiled by Gretchen Zimmer Black With
Irene Burk Harrell

Fleming H. Revell Company
Old Tappan, New Jersey

Unless otherwise identified, Scripture quotations are from the King James Version of the Bible.

Scripture quotations identified NAS are from the New American Standard Bible, © The Lockman Foundation 1960, 1962, 1963, 1968, 1971, 1972, 1973, 1975, 1977.

Scripture quotations identified NIV are from the HOLY BIBLE: NEW INTERNATIONAL VERSION, Copyright © 1978 by the New York International Bible Society. Used by permission of Zondervan Bible Publishers.

Scripture quotations identified RSV are from the Revised Standard Version of the Bible, copyrighted 1946, 1952, © 1971 and 1973.

Scripture quotations identified TAB are from the Amplified New Testament, © The Lockman Foundation 1954, 1958.

Scripture quotations identified TEV are from the *Good News Bible*—Old Testament: Copyright © American Bible Society 1976: New Testament: Copyright © American Bible Society 1966, 1971, 1976.

Scripture quotations identified TLB are from The Living Bible, copyright © 1971 by Tyndale House Publishers, Wheaton, IL. Used by permission.

This book was originally published by Logos International as *Instant Answers for King's Kids in Training.* This is a revised, updated, and expanded edition.

Library of Congress Cataloging in Publication Data

Hill, Harold, 1905–
Bible answers for King's kids.

Rev., updated, and expanded ed. of: Instant answers for King's kids in training. c1978.
1. Christian life—Biblical teaching.   2. Christian life—Quotations, maxims, etc.   I. Black, Gretchen Zimmer.   II. Harrell, Irene Burke.   III. Title.
BS2545.C48H54   1984   248.4   83-9634
ISBN 0-8007-5131-0

Directions for the Use of the Bible Answers Book

Hi King's Kids!

Here's what you've been waiting for ... a whole bookful of *Bible Answers* to just about everything that can happen to you today ... dozens of solutions ... right at your fingertips.

What's your problem? Is it related to Business ... Emotions ... Family ... Travel ... Habits ... Health ... Money ... People ... Religion ... Drinking Too Much ... Husband-Wife Haggles ...? Or is it simply a Mixed and Matched Bag of other Assorted Woes?

Whatever your problem, you know that God has all the answers. But sometimes, the answers are hard to find. That's where *Bible Answers* comes in.

Bible Answers offers help in a hurry. Instead of rooting through sixty-six Bible books plus a concordance or two, you can simply follow the directions and be quickly on your way rejoicing and praising God for His goodness to His young'uns.

Remember, God is no respecter of persons. What He has done for one, He will do for all. Here's how to find what He has done for you:

1. Find your problem, or one like it, in the *Bible Answers* book. It's all alphabetically arranged, just like the dictionary.
2. Read God's answer to the problem in the Scriptures printed below your problem.
3. Read my comments and mini-report.
4. For further details about how it works for me, turn to the relevant King's kid report as indexed in my other seven books: *King's Kid* (*How to Live Like a King's Kid*), *Goo* (*How Did It All Begin? From Goo to You by Way of the Zoo*), *Winner* (*How to Be a*

5

Winner), *Victory* (*How to Live in High Victory*), *Flab* (*How to Flip Your Flab—Forever*), *Live the Bible* (*How to Live the Bible Like a King's Kid*), and *God's in Charge* (*God's in Charge Here*). Numbers refer to pages in the books to which reference is made.

Simple enough? That's all there is to it, but here are some further hints for best results:

1. Get a really solid handle on the Word of God and refuse to be impressed by appearances. Soak in the truth of Romans 8:28 in *every* situation: "And we KNOW that all things work together for good to them that love God, to them who are the called according to his purpose." (That's talking about real King's kids, all right.)
2. Make certain you have no hidden roadblocks such as unforgiveness, impatience, unbelief, resentments, and their scroungy relatives which are always trying to hinder or block the arrival of answers to prayer.
3. Detach emotionally from ownership of the problem by praising Jesus, the new owner to whom you have transferred title.
4. Do NOT be a clock-watcher (2 Peter 3:9; Hebrews 12:1). Allow God a reasonable amount of time. Remember how long it took you to get into that mess by your own very best efforts!
5. Watch carefully for the answer . . . it may appear in a totally unexpected manner . . . far better than anything you could have dreamed up yourself.

According to Romans 10:17 in the *Manufacturer's Handbook,* "Faith cometh by hearing, and hearing by the word of God" in action in the lives of other King's kids who have tried it and reported how it works for them.

Drop me a line c/o King's Kids' Korner, P.O. Box 8655, Baltimore, MD, 21240, and let me know how these *Bible Answers* work for you.

Harold Hill, Reporter
King's Kid in Training

P.S. The *Bible Answers* book is good for something else, too. It's a King's Kid Concordance. To quickly locate a particular incident in any one of the first seven King's kid books, simply look under a key word in the *Bible Answers* book . . . **Mercedes-Benz; Missing Day; Muscle Spasms,** and so on. Happy Hunting.

BIBLE ANSWERS
for
KING'S KIDS

ABC's for King's Kids, God's in Charge 144–46
Accidents. See **Broken Bones; Highway Accidents**
Adam and Eve, Goo 51–56; Victory 40–41, 297; Flab 20–23, 36, 63; God's in Charge 18, 106–7
Additives, Flab 65–74
Adversity. See **Praise in Adversity; Troubles**

Air Travel Problems

God's answer: Rejoice evermore. Pray without ceasing. In every thing give thanks: for this is the will of God in Christ Jesus concerning you. (1 Thessalonians 5:16–18)

Yes, be bold and strong! Banish fear and doubt! For remember, the Lord your God is with you wherever you go. (Joshua 1:9 TLB)

And we know that all things work together for good to them that love God, to them who are the called according to his purpose. (Romans 8:28)

Rest in the Lord, and wait patiently for him. (Psalms 37:7a)

Comments and mini-report: Can God fix an airplane in midair? If not, I'm a dead King's kid.

The trip from Bermuda had been smooth and uneventful until suddenly a voice boomed over the intercom, "Brace yourselves for a belly landing—our landing gear won't come down."

"Hallelujah, Lord!" I prayed. "This sure looks like graduation day has arrived. Just make it quick and easy."

How did God deliver? Miraculously! Read all about it in *King's Kid* 1–6.

Further King's kid reports about air travel problems that turned into testimonies: *King's Kid* 139–42;

11

Winner 113–15, 151–57; *Live the Bible* 69–71: *God's in Charge* 98–99.

Alanon Family Groups

God's answer: Bear ye one another's burdens, and so fulfil the law of Christ. (Galatians 6:2)

Let us be concerned for one another, to help one another to show love and to do good. Let us not give up the habit of meeting together, as some are doing. Instead, let us encourage one another all the more. . . . (Hebrews 10:24–25 TEV)

Blessed be God, even the Father of our Lord Jesus Christ, the Father of mercies, and the God of all comfort; Who comforteth us in all our tribulation, that we may be able to comfort them which are in any trouble, by the comfort wherewith we ourselves are comforted of God. (2 Corinthians 1:3–4)

Comments and mini-report: Do you have a loved one who drinks too much? Are you baffled by the strange behavior of an otherwise caring person who suddenly becomes violent and irrational? Do you insist that willpower is the answer? Of course you do, unless you're ready for *real* help with the problem. In fact, if you are the spouse of a souse—or even a friend—the Alanon Family Groups can assist you in a lifesaving experience.

Located just about everywhere, Alanon Family Groups can help to answer many questions concerning this family disease called alcoholism. Read more about it in *Victory* 1–10.

Alcohol. See **Drinking Too Much**

Angels

God's answer: For he shall give his angels charge over thee, to keep thee in all thy ways. (Psalms 91:11)

What are the angels, then? They are spirits who serve God and are sent by him to help those who are to receive salvation. (Hebrews 1:14 TEV)

Comments and mini-report: Are angels available nowadays to help get King's kids out of messes? Of course. Have I ever experienced such things? Yes, many times.

Being mired in quicksand up to my eyeballs—and still sinking—I'd have been only a bubble on the surface if God hadn't sent a couple of angels.

Being stuck in a traffic jam with no way out to make a flight connection in time could have been a disaster—without angelic help.

Or being stuck in a blizzard many miles from town, *without* food and *with* an empty fuel tank.

You can read all about these three dilemmas in *King's Kid* 18–22 (the quicksand); *Winner* 85–93 (the traffic jam); and *Victory* 303–8 (the blizzard). And there's an account of another angel in *Victory* 309–12.

Still not satisfied that angels are for real? Maybe you'd be persuaded if you knew about the three white angelic vehicles that appeared out of nowhere when I needed them. Or about the money-changing angel who came to help me out in the German restaurant just in time to keep me from being flung into the local hoosegow. These angels-to-the-rescue accounts appear in *Live the Bible* 60–62 and 109–12.

Angels of Light

God's answer: And no marvel; for Satan himself is transformed into an angel of light. Therefore it is no great thing if his ministers also be transformed as the ministers of righteousness; whose end shall be according to their works. (2 Corinthians 11:14–15)

Comments and mini-report: Did you have the idea that Satan generally appears dressed in dirty red snuggies, dragging a moth-eaten forked tail? Not so. Slue Foot's best trick is to appear as a real heavenly being, dressed in enough truth to deceive all but the fully equipped King's kids who know all about these things.

Do you know how to tell the real from the counterfeit? At one time I didn't, and it cost me a whole lot. In fact, this very day, in churches everywhere, the enemy is active through numerous error groups, breaking up families and destroying homes. Become familiar with these things for your own well-being and safety.

For one case history, read *Victory* 281–92.

Anger

God's answer: If you are angry, don't sin by nursing your grudge. Don't let the sun go down with you still angry—get over it quickly; for when you are angry you give a mighty foothold to the devil. (Ephesians 4:26–27 TLB)

The fool who provokes his family to anger and resentment will finally have nothing worthwhile left. (Proverbs 11:29 TLB)

Wherefore, my beloved brethren, let every man be swift to hear, slow to speak, slow to wrath: For the wrath of man worketh not the righteousness of God. (James 1:19–20)

Comments and mini-report: Behind every angry outburst lies an insecure person trying to appear important and not doing very well at it. His Royal Highness, King Brat, simply must be the center of attention, even if it takes a temper tantrum which really impresses no one.

Anger requires more energy output than any other emotion and is therefore totally devastating to the one who practices it.

Until I forgave my former business partner for stealing a large sum of money from me, my anger caused nervous tension, loss of sleep, and poor digestion. When I forgave him, I was set free, and all systems were "Go" again.

Read all about it in *Winner* 79–83. And there's more about anger and its effects in *Victory* 192–204; *Goo* 62; *Live the Bible* 53–57.

Anorexia Nervosa

God's answer: Therefore take no thought, saying, What shall we eat? or, What shall we drink? . . . for your heavenly Father knoweth that ye have need of all these things. But seek ye first the kingdom of God, and his righteousness; and all these things shall be added unto you. (Matthew 6:31–33)

Whether therefore ye eat, or drink, or whatsoever ye do, do all to the glory of God. (1 Corinthians 10:31)

Comments and mini-report: Anorexia is bad stuff. It can get fatal in a hurry. But when the anorexic has a friend who knows how to praise the Lord, the story can have a happy ending. In Katie's case, it was her ever-lovin' grandma who got on her prayer bones and changed the course of events before it was too late. You can read all about it in *Live the Bible* 121–22. And see *Flab* 139–40.

Anti-Mudites

God's answer: Now I beseech you, brethren, mark them which cause divisions and offences contrary to the doctrine which ye have learned; and avoid them. (Romans 16:17)

Now I beseech you, brethren, by the name of our Lord Jesus Christ, that ye all speak the same thing, and that there be no divisions among you; but that ye be perfectly joined together in the same mind and in the same judgment. (1 Corinthians 1:10)

Comments and mini-report: What are Anti-Mudites? The opposite of Mudites, of course! And what is this all about? It's about the difference between religion and spirituality.

Religion depends on good behavior, eating the right things, wearing or not wearing certain apparel—in general, depending on man-made doctrines for assurance of salvation and eternal life.

Religiosity says, "If you don't believe as I do, you're a loser."

We Southern Baptists have about as many types and varieties of religious doctrines as there are pickles, and confronting doctrines different from ours produces in us the facial expression of the chief taster in a pickle factory—a *sour* pickle factory.

Read all about the absurdity of it all in *Victory* 115–17.

Anxiety (see also Stress)

God's answer: Casting all your care upon him; for he careth for you. (1 Peter 5:7)

And besides, what's the use of worrying? What good does it do? Will it add a single day to your life? Of course not! He will always give you all you need from day to day if you will make the Kingdom of God your primary concern. (Luke 12:25, 31 TLB)

Don't worry about anything; instead, pray about everything; tell God your needs and don't forget to thank him for his answers. (Philippians 4:6 TLB)

Comments and mini-report: Uncertainty is most often the cause of a nerve-racking attitude called anxiety. When allowed to dominate the attention for any length of time, anxiety ends in many kinds of fear and eventually causes total immobility.

"Be careful [*anxious* NIV] for nothing" (Philippians 4:6) is easy to say to the distraught person, but without an effective antidote, it's of little comfort.

I got into an anxiety trap at one time in my life which caused me to actually lose consciousness of my surroundings and nearly made me a nervous wreck. Then Jesus Christ came into my life and put an end to that awful killer—anxiety. I learned that Jesus is the only effective antidote.

Read more about anxiety and its results in *Goo* 63, 76; *Winner* 135–41; *Victory* 107; *Live the Bible* 39–40, 97–100, 121–22.

Appetites, Flab 17–43
Apple Pie, Victory 99–103
Aristotle, King's Kid 20

Armor of God
God's answer: Wherefore take unto you the whole armour of God, that ye may be able to withstand in the evil day, and having done all, to stand. Stand therefore, having your loins girt about with truth, and having on the breastplate of righteousness; And your feet shod with the preparation of the gospel of peace;

Above all, taking the shield of faith, wherewith ye shall be able to quench all the fiery darts of the wicked. And take the helmet of salvation, and the sword of the Spirit, which is the word of God. (Ephesians 6:13–17)

Comments and mini-report: Ignorance of the way God's programs work, according to the *Manufacturer's Handbook,* robs King's kids of blessings and victories which are rightly ours, being provided for through God's promises and our inheritance in Jesus. Likewise, protection from enemy attack is available to us, but it does not come through accident or without personal action on our part.

Taking on the full armor of God is a deliberate, careful thing. Carelessness leads to hit-or-miss results.

There is a piece of protective equipment available for the protection of all our vital organs, including protection from mind invasion by demonic forces. And there are weapons of spiritual warfare with which we can come against all the powers of darkness.

Do you know how to apply this armor of God? If not, learn now, and stop settling for second best.

Read all about this armor and these weapons in *Goo* 75; *Winner* 71–77, 175–88; *God's in Charge* 139.

Arthritis

God's answer: Be not wise in thine own eyes: fear the Lord, and depart from evil. It shall be health to thy navel, and marrow to thy bones. (Proverbs 3:7–8)

When I pray, you answer me, and encourage me by giving me the strength I need. (Psalms 138:3 TLB)

Confess your faults one to another, and pray one for another, that ye may be healed. (James 5:16a)

Comments and mini-report: My arthritic shoulder had been anointed with enough oil to fill ten dozen crankcases; more dozens of demons had been cast out with repeated loud exhortations; and still my shoulder grew worse. Finally, after four years of increasing misery—to the point where I could barely raise my arm high enough to put on my coat—I followed the procedure set forth in the *Manufacturer's Handbook* and got instant healing.

Prayer, anointing, exhortation, and medical science all have their part in God's plan for healing His people. But broken relationships, people-to-people, must be dealt with eyeball-to-eyeball or the results will be negative.

Doing the Bible thing, I discovered something: It works! I'm healed, praise God. Try God's method on *your* arthritis!

For more about arthritis—and the attitudes that bring it on, read *King's Kid* 108–11, 199–213; *Goo* 77–78; *Winner* 82–83; *Victory* 192–94; *God's in Charge* 158.

Just about the most amazing case of healing from arthritis that has ever reached my ears is the story of Kay Golbeck, who was hospitalized for eight and a half years with the disease. What happened when she did the Bible thing and called for the elders of the church to anoint her with oil? Wow! Now, there's a miracle that will bless you out of your socks. Read about her in *Live the Bible* 120–21.

Atoms

God's answer: For by him were all things created, that are in heaven, and that are in earth, visible and invisible, whether they be thrones, or dominions, or principalities, or powers: all things were created by him, and for him: And he is before all things, and by him all things consist. (Colossians 1:16–17)

Comments and mini-report: Knowledge of how God assembled and maintains His universe is helpful in answering many of life's questions. When your child asks, "Did we really descend from apes, like my teacher says, or is God my real heavenly Father?" you'll give him the "Run along—can't you see I'm busy right now?" brush-off unless you are armed with the facts.

Is the earth really billions of years old, as the evolutionists say—or is God's account of a relatively young earth right? Did we all descend from a common little glob of goo? Is all flesh related by heredity—or are all types specially created for specific purpose in God's master plan?

Get all the up-to-date facts so you can shoot down evolution's subtle lies. Learn how God will ultimately restructure all atoms into a brand-new heaven and earth. You can get acquainted with atoms in *Goo* 60, 61, 80–81.

Attendance, Miserable

God's answer: For where two or three are gathered together in my name, there am I in the midst of them. (Matthew 18:20)

Comments and mini-report: What constitutes a successful meeting? Large numbers of raised hands and scores of signed commitment cards? Maybe. But God can do a lot with a little. In reality, it takes only two people to make a meeting—one to talk and one to listen.

The businessmen's Monday-morning prayer group had dwindled to the point where there were just two of us—my friend Ed and myself. Common sense dictated, "Disband it! God has finished with this group; it's served its purpose. Time to quit." Ed and I agreed—but we just seemed to be drawn back each week.

Then one day a stranger walked in and got saved!

Maybe you have about decided your efforts for God are in vain. Read how we almost blew it and how the Holy Spirit kept us steady and faithful in spite of appearances. The report is in *Victory* 205–11.

Attitudes. See **Brooding; Negative Confession**
Authority. See **Rebellion**

Automatic Writing

God's answer: Beloved, believe not every spirit, but try the spirits whether they are of God: because many false prophets are gone out into the world. Hereby know ye the Spirit of God: Every spirit that confesseth that Jesus Christ is come in the flesh is of God. (1 John 4:1–2)

Comments and mini-report: Can demon spirits actually communicate with people on paper? Of course. I've seen it happen many times. In fact, I depended on this communication for technical answers to problems for years before I was saved.

The enemy uses many tricks to trap folks into his kingdom of darkness, and spirit writing is one of them.

My wife grew up in a home where such practices were a part of everyday living. Ouija boards, seances, and medium activities were accepted as being right from God. Then Satan sprung his trap, and for many months I had no wife—just a mentally ill patient in an asylum. Our "friends," the familiar spirits mentioned

21

in the Bible as an abomination to God, had taken over.

Was there a way out? Only through Jesus Christ and the power gifts of the Holy Spirit. Read all about my wife's deliverance in *King's Kid* 179–84.

Backbiting. See **Tongue Trouble**

Back Trouble
God's answer: He sent his word, and healed them, and delivered them from their destructions. (Psalms 107:20)

Beloved, I wish above all things that thou mayest prosper and be in health, even as thy soul prospereth. (3 John 2)

And these signs shall follow them that believe; they shall lay hands on the sick, and they shall recover. (Mark 16:17a, 18b)

Comments and mini-report: "Disintegration of the fifth lumbar disk" was essentially what the medical report told me about the misery I had suffered for many years prior to my checkup.

"Paralysis within two years if you don't have surgery," the doctor said when I asked the prognosis. That didn't sound too good, so I asked another question: "Do you guarantee good results from surgery?" "We do our medical best," he shrugged, "but a fifty-fifty chance of recovery is the most we can offer."

I wanted better odds than that, so God's statement in Mark 16:17 began to look mighty attractive. I had been saved and had begun to take the *Manufacturer's Handbook* as being written especially for me as a King's kid in training. But there were still complications. For instance, my pastor, a Southern Baptist theologian, said, "No way!" when I asked him about it. "That all went out of style when the disciples died off," he explained.

But I couldn't take his word for it—my back hurt too bad. And so I stood in a healing line and got healed anyway. Praise God! Read about my healing in *King's Kid* 39–43. And read about the healing of a Methodist's bad back in *Victory* 99–103.

Bad debts. See **Debts**
Bad Things, Live the Bible, 119–26; God's in Charge 18, 26–33, 115–19, 148–50, 154–56, 159
Banquets, Victory 263–64

Baptism in the Holy Spirit (see also **Power Shortage)**
God's answer: Repent, and be baptized every one of you in the name of Jesus Christ for the remission of sins, and ye shall receive the gift of the Holy Ghost. (Acts 2:38)

Behold the Lamb of God, which taketh away the sin of the world . . . the same is he which baptizeth with the Holy Ghost. (John 1:29b, 33b)

If ye then, being evil, know how to give good gifts unto your children: how much more shall your heavenly Father give the Holy Spirit to them that ask him? (Luke 11:13)

(For as yet he was fallen upon none of them: only they were baptized in the name of the Lord Jesus.) Then laid they their hands on them, and they received the Holy Ghost. (Acts 8:16–17)

Have ye received the Holy Ghost since ye believed? (Acts 19:2a)

Comments and mini-report: Is the Baptism in the Holy Spirit received at the time of salvation?

Do we "get it all" at that time, or is there more?

Is the Baptism of Jesus the same as the Baptism of the Holy Spirit?

Confusion is rampant today on account of ignorance of the Bible's answers to these questions. To get it all straight in your mind, read *King's Kid* 45–58, 65; *Goo* 83–86; *Winner* 15–26, 75–77; *Victory* 83–89, 250–52; *God's in Charge* 87–88.

Baptism, Water

God's answer: For as many of you as have been baptized into Christ have put on Christ. (Galatians 3:27)

Therefore we are buried with him by baptism into death: that like as Christ was raised up from the dead by the glory of the Father, even so we also should walk in newness of life. (Romans 6:4)

And as they went on their way, they came unto a certain water: and the eunuch said, See, here is water; what doth hinder me to be baptized? And Philip said, If thou believest with all thine heart, thou mayest. And he answered and said, I believe that Jesus Christ is the Son of God. (Acts 8:36–37)

He that believeth and is baptized shall be saved. (Mark 16:16a)

In Him also you were circumcised with a circumcision not made with hands, but in a (spiritual) circumcision (performed by) Christ by stripping off the body of the flesh (the whole corrupt, carnal nature with its passions and lusts). (Thus you were circumcised when) you were buried with Him in (your) baptism, in which

24

you were also raised with Him (to a new life) through (your) faith in the working of God (as displayed) when He raised Him up from the dead. (Colossians 2:11–12 TAB)

Comments and mini-report: Many King's kids are confused by such questions as:

Is water baptism necessary for salvation?

Should I be immersed completely or is it okay to be spattered, sprinkled, or poured upon?

What are the proper words for the pastor to use? Should he say, "In the name of Jesus"? Or should he say, "In the name of the Father, Son, and Holy Ghost"? Or should he say something else entirely? Just what is right?

After I was saved in 1954 and heard about the total-immersion ceremony used in my church, I began to ask such questions, with a few more added to the list:

Wasn't the baptism I received as a child sufficient? Must I be immersed to be certain of being right with God?

My wife, an Episcopal lady, began asking the same questions after she was saved.

"Ask and it shall be given," Jesus said. Sure enough, as we began to ask, God taught us the best answers. Heaven's best is always available for King's kids who know how to get it.

Read all about water baptism in *King's Kid* 25, 45–46, 49–51; *Goo* 66; *Victory* 164–65.

Bathsheba. See **David and Bathsheba**

Bathtub, Parable of the
God's answer: Let that therefore abide in you, which ye have heard from the beginning. If that which ye have heard from the beginning shall remain in you, ye

also shall continue in the Son, and in the Father. (1 John 2:24)

Comments and mini-report: The heavenly joy and pure ecstasy of the Baptism in the Holy Spirit were no longer with me that miserable morning when I awoke. And Satan was quick to whisper, "You see? God has given up on you. You're just too much for Him to handle."

For an instant, I panicked. Then came the Word of the Lord to my rescue: "I will never leave you nor forsake you."

"Thank You, Jesus," I said. "But what's happened to all those delicious feelings I've had since You baptized me in Your Holy Spirit?"

Then the Lord taught me a profound truth about these things through the Parable of the Bathtub—full of hot water. And that left old Slue Foot in plenty of the same!

Read all about it in *Victory* 25–30.

Bedmates

God's answer: Not that I speak in respect of want: for I have learned, in whatsoever state I am, therewith to be content. (Philippians 4:11)

Comments and mini-report: What would *you* do under these circumstances:
1) You arrive at a town to minister with Tommy Tyson for a week.
2) Your hostess assigns you both to the same bed.
3) The bed is not a double bed; it's three-quarter size.
4) You and Tommy weigh well over 200 pounds apiece.
5) It's midwinter in the Michigan farmhouse attic

where the bed is shoved against the well-ventilated eaves.

6) Your bedmate rolls himself up in all the covers, leaving you to freeze solid unless you stay alert.

Well, I don't know what *you* would have done, but as for me, I prayed—harder.

Situations like that really improve your prayer life—especially when you know you're stuck with the arrangement for a week and the attic will remain unheated.

To see how God turned that set of circumstances into something that worked for good, read *Victory* 118–20.

Bellyaching

God's answer: In every thing give thanks: for this is the will of God in Christ Jesus concerning you. (1 Thessalonians 5:18)

Do everything without complaining or arguing, so that you may become blameless and pure, children of God without fault in a crooked and depraved generation, in which you shine like stars in the universe as you hold out the word of life. . . . (Philippians 2:14–16 NIV)

Comments and mini-report: Is it possible for a King's kid to praise the Lord through untold agonies for a dozen chapters in a row and then sink to the depths of misery, just like a pagan, when he temporarily gets out of praising gear? You'd better believe it! The day it happened to me, I was the most surprised fellow in the world, but that didn't change the situation, which looked as if it would be terminal any minute. Read up on these things in *Live the Bible* 37–107.

Bias

God's answer: But the man who isn't a Christian can't understand and can't accept these thoughts from God, which the Holy Spirit teaches us. They sound foolish to him, because only those who have the Holy Spirit within them can understand what the Holy Spirit means. Others just can't take it in. But the spiritual man has insight into everything, and that bothers and baffles the man of the world, who can't understand him at all. How could he? For certainly he has never been one to know the Lord's thoughts, or to discuss them with him, or to move the hands of God by prayer. But, strange as it seems, we Christians actually do have within us a portion of the very thoughts and mind of Christ. (1 Corinthians 2:14–16 TLB)

Comments and mini-report: When the Word of God is diluted by human wisdom or commonsense reason, it is biased away from pure Truth and loses its intended effectiveness.

Bias, or man's wisdom, literally closes off receptivity to God's provisions and results finally in the attitude, "God doesn't hear my prayers as He does other folks'."

Bias is used in electronic circuits to completely block all flow of power—and it works that way in spiritual matters, too.

The remedy? Get rid of it.

How? Someone gave me a slogan that helped: K I S S—Keep It Simple, Stupid!

For more about bias, read *Goo* 73–75 and *Victory* 88–89.

Bible. See **Manufacturer's Handbook**
Big-Shot-Itis. See **Self-Reliance**

Billy-Goat Christians

God's answer: I know thy works, that thou art neither cold nor hot: I would thou wert cold or hot. So then because thou art lukewarm, and neither cold nor hot, I will spue thee out of my mouth. (Revelation 3:15–16)

Beware lest any man spoil you through philosophy and vain deceit, after the tradition of men, after the rudiments of the world, and not after Christ. (Colossians 2:8)

Comments and mini-report: Now and then someone writes, complaining about the title of my first book, *How to Live Like a King's Kid.* Some have asked, "Why not refer to us as King's lambs?"

"How about it, Lord?" I asked, the first time this came up.

God seemed to reply, "When my people stop saying, 'Yes, but—' and begin saying, 'Yes, Lord,' they will sound more like lambs than billy goats. Until then—"

I was satisfied the title He had given me for the book was justified.

Are you a "yes, but"child of the King?

Further information about billy-goat Christians can be found in *Goo* 72; *Victory* 83–89; *Live the Bible* 70.

Binding and Loosing

God's answer: Verily I say unto you, Whatsoever ye shall bind on earth shall be bound in heaven: and whatsoever ye shall loose on earth shall be loosed in heaven. (Matthew 18:18)

Comments and mini-report: Did you know that we actually possess the power to bind or loose conditions here on planet earth? Most folks have no idea this is true, although it is clearly stated in the Word of God and I have found it true in my own experience.

My daughter was declared by medical science to be beyond any hope of living through the night. Her condition was desperate—and so was I—and so was my wife.

"Lord, our only child is dying!" we wailed. "Don't You even care?"

After hours of this futile sort of possessive binding prayer, we gave up in total exhaustion. Then the Holy Spirit was able to get our attention and come to the rescue with the truth about this binding and loosing principle.

Learn about it from my experience. It might save the life of your loved one someday. Further details about our daughter's case are in *King's Kid* 152–55. More reading about the binding and loosing principle can be found in *King's Kid* 96, 207–9; *Winner* xviii, 85–93; *Victory* 106–7; *Live the Bible* 50, 78–79, 115.

Binding power. See **Atoms**

Blabbermouths

God's answer: Wherefore, my beloved brethren, let every man be swift to hear, slow to speak, slow to wrath. (James 1:19)

And the servant of the Lord must not strive; but must be gentle unto all men, apt to teach, patient, In meekness instructing those that oppose themselves. (2 Timothy 2:24–25a)

But the tongue can no man tame. (James 3:8a)

Comments and mini-report: Remember that after you first got filled with the Holy Spirit you wanted to run out and tell everybody all about it? Not only that, you wanted to crowd them into a corner and keep them hemmed up there until they had an experience exactly like yours?

Funny—they didn't seem interested. Worse than that, after a while, it seemed as if your best friends had become somebody else's best friends and they all ganged up to avoid you at all costs.

Blabbermouth-itis. It can happen to newly turned-on Christians, all right. And it seems to turn everybody else off.

What to do about this problem? Does the *Manufacturer's Handbook* have anything to suggest? Of course! Read all about it in *Winner* 21–26; *Victory* 66.

Blahs. See **Emptiness**
Blindness. See **Eyeball Ailments**

Blizzards
God's answer: For he hath said, I will never leave thee, nor forsake thee. (Hebrews 13:5b)

I pray that you will begin to understand how incredibly great his power is to help those who believe him. (Ephesians 1:19 TLB)

Comments and mini-report: As I drove across North Carolina that winter day, the unexpected blizzard raged, and the snow drifted and piled higher and higher. Along toward noon, all traffic ground to a halt. Trucks jackknifed and cars double-laned themselves into a mass of metal and panic. Me? Caught in the midst of it, I continued to praise the Lord for His goodness and mercy—at first.

31

But after a while, appearances got the best of my prayer life, and I began to join the critics.

"Lord, it looks as if You've let me down, hard. There's just no way out of freezing to death before the night is over," I wailed. "Please, Lord. How about a miracle like the one You worked for Paul and Silas when You sent an angel to open their prison doors?"

Do you think He heard me? And how! Read all about it in *Victory* 303–8. Further blizzardly adventures are recounted in *Winner* 55–61; *Victory* 11–17.

Blown Minds

God's answer: The whole head is sick. (Isaiah 1:5)

But the natural man receiveth not the things of the Spirit of God: for they are foolishness unto him: neither can he know them, because they are spiritually discerned. (1 Corinthians 2:14)

That ye put off concerning the former conversation the old man, which is corrupt according to the deceitful lusts; And be renewed in the spirit of your mind; And that ye put on the new man, which after God is created in righteousness and true holiness. (Ephesians 4:22–24)

Comments and mini-report: Before you were saved, did anyone ever tell you, "Just read your Bible and you'll be all right?" And didn't it frustrate you almost to death that when you blew the dust off it, the Bible was just a jumble of contradictions and dull words without any meaning?

Do you know why that was necessarily so? Do you know that you arrived on planet earth with a blown mind? Most folks don't know it, but their ignorance doesn't change the truth.

You need to be familiar with these important facts so you can begin to help others into the Kingdom.

You can read about your blown mind in *Goo* 53; *Victory* 40–46.

Blown tires. See **Highway Accidents**

Bomb Shelters

God's answer: For thou hast been a strength to the poor, a strength to the needy in his distress, a refuge from the storm, a shadow from the heat, when the blast of the terrible ones is as a storm against the wall. (Isaiah 25:4)

Comments and mini-report: A while back, when everyone was talking about bomb shelters, my business partner announced plans for an underground shelter at our plant to accommodate all our personnel.

"You'll have quarters here," he told me, indicating a room on the architect's drawings. "And right here," he added, pointing to a wall space, "is a rack for the shotguns."

"Shotguns?" I asked. "Just what would we be shooting underground? Moles, maybe?"

"No, you idiot," he burst forth. "We'll need guns to shoot the neighbors if they try to break in. It'll be every man for himself. If they can't provide for their own safety, they'll be out of luck."

"Forget my space in that cave," I told him. "*I* have a better means of protection than a brick and concrete coffin with all that headroom."

"And just what, may I ask, might that be?" he asked.

Good question. What's *your* answer? What will you do when the bombs start to fall? Will you seek an un-

33

derground hideout and after things cool off come out to a world of burnt neighbors and radioactive ruins? Or will you have a better means of protection?

For God's answer, read *King's Kid* 144–45.

Boob-Tube-Itis

God's answer: If ye then be risen with Christ, seek those things which are above, where Christ sitteth on the right hand of God. (Colossians 3:1)

Every word of God is pure: he is a shield unto them that put their trust in him. (Proverbs 30:5)

Thy word is a lamp unto my feet, and a light unto my path. (Psalms 119:105)

Let the word of Christ dwell in you richly in all wisdom. (Colossians 3:16a)

Now is the judgment of this world: now shall the prince of this world be cast out. And I, if I be lifted up from the earth, will draw all men unto me. (John 12:31–32)

For a man is a slave to whatever controls him. (2 Peter 2:19b TLB)

Comments and mini-report: Recently a Baltimore newscast announced that a ten-year-old boy was being questioned about his motive in killing his five-year-old friend from next door.

"I only did what I saw them doing on TV," he insisted.

Is secular TV programming *your* child to be a murderer?

34

To stir your thinking about your responsibility about these things, read *Goo* 62; *Winner* 147–48; *Victory* 136–39, 300.

Boredom. See **Emptiness**

Born Again, How to Be
God's answer: Jesus answered and said unto him, Verily, verily, I say unto thee, Except a man be born again, he cannot see the kingdom of God. (John 3:3)

Only the Holy Spirit gives eternal life. Those born only once, with physical birth, will never receive this gift. (John 6:63 TLB)

But to all who received him, he gave the right to become children of God. All they needed to do was to trust him to save them. All those who believe this are reborn!—not a physical rebirth resulting from human passion or plan—but from the will of God. (John 1:12–13 TLB)

Comments and mini-report: "No, Nicodemus, you do not undergo another physical birth," paraphrases the words of Jesus to a leading teacher of religion in His day. The Bible account indicates that Nicodemus had the equivalent of his master's degree in theology, yet he had no awareness of spiritual things.

The second birth comes by the Spirit of God, not by human mechanism. That fact baffles all attempts at intellectual understanding by our Educated Idiot Boxes.

My own life was transformed in 1954 when the second birth happened to me. Has the second birth taken place in *your* life?

For instructions on getting born again, read *King's Kid* 18, 23; *Goo* 65–69, 80–83, 89–90; *Winner* 7–14, 195; *Victory* 151; *Flab* 57; *Live the Bible* 31–32; *God's in Charge* 34–39. You guessed it, I've put the directions for new creaturehood in every single one of my books, because being born again is an absolutely indispensable ingredient for King's kid living. If you wanted to be highfalutin, you could call it the sine qua non. But even if you don't go for the Latin, go for being born again—it'll come in handy for all eternity.

Broken Bones

God's answer: We know that all things work together for good to them that love God, to them who are the called according to his purpose. (Romans 8:28)

This sickness is not unto death, but for the glory of God, that the Son of God might be glorified thereby. (John 11:4)

Comments and mini-report: One thing for which I had never felt the slightest need was a broken bone. In fact, I went through over half a century of living without my first one. And I didn't miss it a bit. Then I inadvertently asked for and received not just one, but three at one pop.

How did I happen to ask for three broken bones? By praying amiss, that's how.

Have you ever prayed amiss and things happened that you didn't like? Maybe you never connected the results with the wrong kind of prayer, but I did.

I was simply too busy—I thought—to carry out an assignment the Lord had given me. I was using the time shortage as an alibi. "Lord, if I had more time I would be glad to get that job done for You," I weaseled.

The Lord very obligingly gave me several extra

weeks in various sizes of plaster casts as I recovered from those broken bones for which I had unwittingly signed the order.

Read all about it in *Winner* 27–32—and be careful how *you* pray. For another broken-bone adventure with life-changing results, read *Flab* 13–16. If you're worried about your weight, I can practically guarantee that reading the rest of the book will start you to shrinking—permanently.

Broken Fan Belt, Live the Bible 37–43

Broken Relationships (see also **Divorce; Fractured Marriage)**

God's answer: Therefore if thou bring thy gift to the altar, and there rememberest that thy brother hath ought against thee; Leave there thy gift before the altar, and go thy way; first be reconciled to thy brother, and then come and offer thy gift. (Matthew 5:23–24)

Comments and mini-report: God has designed the human race so that for best results in our lives we must live in harmony with others. This is known in science as the Law of Harmonics, where maximum power flows in circuits which are "in tune."

When we are out of tune with another person, even a little bit, there is a deterioration of God's blessings in our lives and a short-circuiting of nervous energy within the physical system. Hypertension, arthritis, and cancer are only a few of the destructive results of broken relationships.

If these things are true in the physical dimension, how much more do we need to be on guard in our spiritual lives, where our "circuits" are much more sensitive to these things!

If you're still not persuaded, try these King's kids' reports on for size: *King's Kid* 107–11, 200–4; *Victory* 159, 193–94; *Live the Bible* 53–57.

Brooding (see also specific incidents where right brooding made a difference, for example, **Broken Fan Belt; Locked-Up Castle; Charley-Horsed Rib Cage; Golbeck, Kay;** and so on)
God's answer: When God began creating the heavens and the earth, the earth was at first a shapeless, chaotic mass, with the Spirit of God brooding over the dark vapors. (Genesis 1:1–2 TLB)

Comments and mini-report: For what I learned about brooding from a chicken, read *Live the Bible* 15–30.

Buddhism, King's Kid 19
Bugaboos. See **Homosexuality**

Bum Rap
God's answer: Offer unto God thanksgiving; and pay thy vows unto the most High: And call upon me in the day of trouble: I will deliver thee, and thou shalt glorify me. (Psalms 50:14–15)

For what glory is it, if, when ye be buffeted for your faults, ye shall take it patiently? but if, when ye do well, and suffer for it, ye take it patiently, this is acceptable with God. (1 Peter 2:20)

Comments and mini-report: Ask any prison inmate how he got there and more times than not his reply will be "Bum rap. I didn't do it." To hear the inmates tell it, their incarceration is generally someone else's fault.

Sometimes, however, believe it or not, this is really true—but how can the truth help a person already behind bars for a long confinement? The judge's opinion can't be reversed by the judge himself—or can it? Just how would you go about persuading him that he'd made a mistake?

Joe's wife came to the prayer meeting one night in total agony. "This will be our first Thanksgiving Day apart since we've been married," she sobbed. "What can I tell our children to comfort them? *Please* pray that Joe will be home for dinner on Thanksgiving Day."

Everybody knew that, in the natural, such a thing could never happen. But we all knew that King's kids don't have to settle for second best. Could God do something like Joe's wife was asking? Could He persuade the judge he had made the wrong decision? And could He do it in time?

Read all about it in *Winner* 95–100.

Burglary

God's answer: Charge them that are rich in this world, that they be not highminded, nor trust in uncertain riches, but in the living God, who giveth us richly all things to enjoy. (1 Timothy 6:17)

Lay not up for yourselves treasures upon earth, where moth and rust doth corrupt, and where thieves break through and steal: But lay up for yourselves treasures in heaven, where neither moth nor rust doth corrupt, and where thieves do not break through nor steal: For where your treasure is, there will your heart be also. (Matthew 6:19–21)

Comments and mini-report: When we are owners of material things, we are responsible for safeguarding

39

them from thieves, moths, rust, and pollution. But when we become stewards only of God's abundance, then we can look to our heavenly Father to safeguard His possessions.

When you leave your hotel door unlocked—accidentally—as I did, and a burglar creeps in and helps himself to all your valuables—deliberately—what can you do about it?

Relax. If you're a steward instead of an owner, you can expect God to handle the consequences—even a little thing like being penniless in New York City for several days. He handled just such a situation for me—perfectly. Read how in *Winner* 55–58.

For another case history of a burglary that turned out better than a no-burglary, try *Winner* 169–74.

Caleb, Goo 72–73; Victory 32
Calorie Counting, Flab 2–3

Cancer

God's answer: My son, attend to my words; incline thine ear unto my sayings. Let them not depart from thine eyes; keep them in the midst of thine heart. For they are life unto those that find them, and health to all their flesh. (Proverbs 4:20–22)

Bless the Lord, O my soul, and forget not all his benefits: Who forgiveth all thine iniquities; who healeth all thy diseases. (Psalms 103:2–3)

Comments and mini-report: "Why did that beautiful Christian die of that terrible disease?" is a question often heard around the coffin.

"How can God let my loved ones suffer so?" is another unanswered question in hospital waiting rooms.

Why some are healed in the here and now and

40

some continue to linger in torment is absolutely baf-
fling until you realize some of the causes of cancer
and similar ailments. Most folks think these things are
caused by germs or viruses. It never enters their minds
that attitudes have anything to do with the health—or
lack of health—of our physical bodies.

Have you read Dr. Bill Reed's *Surgery of the Soul?*
It could open your eyes to some of these truths. And
Paul Tournier is another who has written many books
revealing the connection between body ailments and
the state of our souls. For some factual reports on
what I've observed about these things, read *King's Kid*
99–102; *Winner* 63–69; *Victory* 63; *God's in Charge*
91–94, 96–97.

Car Trouble (see also **Broken Fan Belt; Highway Accidents; Rental Car Shortage; Traffic**)
God's answer: Offer unto God thanksgiving; and pay
thy vows unto the most High: And call upon me in the
day of trouble: I will deliver thee, and thou shalt
glorify me. (Psalms 50:14–15)

I will praise the Lord no matter what happens.
(Psalms 34:1 TLB)

Great is his faithfulness; his lovingkindness begins
afresh each day. (Lamentations 3:23 TLB)

Comments and mini-report: Suppose you're driving
down a busy highway and suddenly something happens that you've never experienced before—the gear
shift comes right out of the floor and hangs there in
your hand about as useful as a stalk of boiled celery.
Can the promise of God in Romans 8:28 possibly hold
true when horns are blasting at you from every di-

rection, brakes are squealing, and people are hollering things in your direction that aren't fit to print?

Is God able to make a message out of such a mess as that?

And what if the situation is complicated by the fact that it's Saturday afternoon, the car is a foreign car, and you have an out-of-state license? Doesn't that make the situation a sure vehicle for loserhood for all parties concerned?

Not when King's kids praise the Lord! Those very details just happen to match an adventure I had one day, and the outcome included not only a promptly repaired car—with no charge for parts *or* labor—but the bonus benefit of a woman clear across the ocean in Germany being saved and filled with the Holy Spirit!

How could all those happenings fit together? Read all about it in *King's Kid* 125–33 and praise God for the next car trouble *you* are blessed to enjoy.

Castle, Locked-Up

God's answer: ... Behold, I have set before thee an open door, and no man can shut it; for thou hast a little strength, and hast kept my word, and hast not denied my name. (Revelation 3:8)

Comments and mini-report: Have you ever been locked in a castle and the exit key that should have been in your pocket was nowhere to be found? Probably not, I imagine. But you *have* been all sewed up in a comparable situation with no way out, right? In my case, I'd have been a goner for sure if it hadn't been for my partner, who remembered to praise the Lord when I forgot to do it. That fall from grace put me in the worst misery of my entire life! Read all about it in *Live the Bible* 89–104.

Catastrophes. (See **Bad Things** and specific catastrophes, for example, **Arthritis; Blindness; Cancer;
Car Trouble; Debts; Divorce; Highway Accidents,** and
so on)

Cayce, Edgar

God's answer: Enter ye in at the strait gate: for wide is
the gate, and broad is the way, that leadeth to destruction, and many there be which go in thereat: Because
strait is the gate and narrow is the way, which leadeth
unto life, and few there be that find it. Beware of false
prophets, which come to you in sheep's clothing, but
inwardly they are ravening wolves. Ye shall know
them by their fruits. (Matthew 7:13–16a)

Comments and mini-report: "I don't see a thing wrong
with all that Edgar Cayce business" is an insistent
comment I often hear from God's people who are not
aware of the hazards of dabbling in such things. "I
really believe he was a Spirit-filled Christian," some
people persist.

Well, maybe he was. I can't check with him personally because he's graduated to—wherever. But I *can*
report on some of his followers and what they stand
for because I have personally investigated them.

Have you ever heard the name of the god of the
Cayce movement? I have.

Have you ever seen demons eyeball-to-eyeball in a
religious meeting? I have—and it's an experience I'll
never forget. Brrrr!

You can read about it in *Winner* 175–88. Further
comments on the Edgar Cayce cult are in *King's Kid*
21, 182.

Chaff

God's answer: Whose fan is in his hand, and he will thoroughly purge his floor, and gather his wheat into the garner; but he will burn up the chaff with unquenchable fire. (Matthew 3:12)

The ungodly are not so: but are like the chaff which the wind driveth away. (Psalms 1:4)

Comments and mini-report: Is chaff sinful? Not at all. In fact, it's impossible to produce a single grain of wheat without raising a whole lot of chaff—straw, hulls, and other accessories to the growing heads of grain.

But when bread-making time comes, the chaff is in the way. It has to be separated from the wheat if the bread is to be fit to eat.

So it is in the life of a King's kid. There are numerous things which are okay in the beginning of the Christian life—but later on they are like chaff. They need to be disposed of if God is to use us to feed His children.

Does the grain struggle to get rid of the chaff? Or does the Lord of the harvest take care of it?

Do King's kids have to agonize about their "character defects and shortcomings"? Or does the Holy Spirit take charge of the cleansing process?

At Calvary, Jesus said, "It is finished." What does that mean for you? Does it set you free—from anything?

For more about these things, read *Victory* 125–27.

Chickens and Eggs, Live the Bible 15–19
Cholesterol, Flab 64

Christian Science

God's answer: For many deceivers are entered into the world, who confess not that Jesus Christ is come in the flesh. This is a deceiver and an antichrist. Look to yourselves, that we lose not those things which we have wrought, but that we receive a full reward. Whosoever transgresseth, and abideth not in the doctrine of Christ, hath not God. He that abideth in the doctrine of Christ, he hath both the Father and the Son. (2 John 7–9)

Comments and mini-report: When I heard that a famous Christian Science leader had died a violent death, someone remarked, "But I thought God took better care of His servants than that."

The answer is, of course, that He does. And when you realize that Christian Science is neither Christian nor scientific and that God is not in it, that makes a whole world of difference!

"How can you make such a statement?" I hear you sputter.

I have proof of these things, and you need it, too— so that you will no longer be deceived.

Read King's kid reports in *King's Kid* 19, 182; *Victory* 295; *God's in Charge* 73.

Church Membership

God's answer: And all things are of God, who hath reconciled us to himself by Jesus Christ, and hath given to us the ministry of reconciliation. (2 Corinthians 5:18)

For God is not the author of confusion, but of peace, as in all churches of the saints. (1 Corinthians 14:33)

And they, continuing daily with one accord in the temple, and breaking bread from house to house, did eat their meat with gladness and singleness of heart, Praising God, and having favour with all the people. And the Lord added to the church daily such as should be saved. (Acts 2:46–47)

Nor forsaking the assembling of ourselves together, as the manner of some is; but exhorting one another: and so much the more, as ye see the day approaching. (Hebrews 10:25)

Comments and mini-report: "I can worship just as well at home as in a particular building at a particular time and place," say many folks these days.

"My prayer group is my church," others are insisting.

"Who needs a pastor? Why, I'm closer to God than he is," I hear now and then from the uninformed.

What's wrong with all these statements? Do we really need to belong to an organized church group?

It all depends. Do you want heaven's best? Or are you willing to settle for less?

To see how these things work, read *King's Kid* 142–44; *Victory* 121–22, 284.

Cirrhosis of the Liver

God's answer: Heal me, O Lord, and I shall be healed; save me, and I shall be saved: for thou art my praise. (Jeremiah 17:14)

But he was wounded for our transgressions, he was bruised for our iniquities: the chastisement of our peace was upon him; and with his stripes we are healed. (Isaiah 53:5)

Comments and mini-report: "Incurable," the doctor told old Brother Tom as he finished the physical examination. "You drank too much alcohol, you've ruined your liver, and the damage, I'm sorry to say, is irreversible."

Tom was sorry, too. He had just gotten saved and was eager to live awhile longer now that Jesus had taken charge of his life, which had been such a drag before. After seventy-five years of awful emptiness, he was excited, thinking about how Jesus could use him. But now—the death sentence.

"Do you think Jesus can heal cirrhosis?" he asked that night at the prayer meeting.

"There's one sure way to find out," was our answer. "Let's ask Him."

"But the doctor says it's incurable—that the damage is irreversible," Tom continued.

Who was right? Is God able to do the impossible?

Ask Tom! If you can't do that, read all about it in *Winner* 101–6. And you can go on to read about Harry's cirrhosis in *Winner* 191–93.

Claiming the Promises (see also **Doers of the Word**)

God's answer: For all the promises of God in him are yea, and in him Amen, unto the glory of God by us. (2 Corinthians 1:20)

God is not a man, that he should lie; neither the son of man, that he should repent: hath he said, and shall he not do it? or hath he spoken, and shall he not make it good? (Numbers 23:19)

Comments and mini-report: Human wisdom limits our intake of information to the evidence of our five senses. It leaves us with nothing beyond what can be perceived through the areas of seeing, hearing, feeling, smelling, and tasting.

God's wisdom, on the other hand, is limited only to God Himself, who is infinite and whose promises are for us today if we know how to go about realizing them.

Just how can His promises be appropriated into our lives? Simple. We become doers of the Word instead of hearers only.

How is any promise checked for its validity? Test it and look at the results. In the case of God's promises set down in the *Manufacturer's Handbook*, we are to read them and act as if they are true. We are to be obedient to the methods He recommends by acting as if we think they will work.

"Too simple," you say? "If it's all that easy, why don't more folks try it?"

They're biased against it, that's why, because they rely on their minds, not knowing that they were blown in the Garden of Eden. But we don't have to act as if we know more than God. There is a better way. Read all about how claiming the promises of God works in *King's Kid* 150–51; *Victory* 107; *Live the Bible* 11–126.

Claustrophobia, Live the Bible 95–99
Clay. See **Potter and the Clay**
Coma, King's Kid 103

Common Sense
God's answer: Why should ye be stricken any more? ye will revolt more and more: the whole head is sick, and the whole heart faint. (Isaiah 1:5)

For my thoughts are not your thoughts, neither are your ways my ways, saith the Lord. (Isaiah 55:8)

Comments and mini-report: "And just what is wrong with common sense?" asks the human intellect. "God gave it to us—He must have meant for us to use it. Didn't He?"

The answer is, of course, that nothing is wrong with common sense as long as it is properly related to the Word of God and His instructions for its proper usage.

What does God have to say about these things? A lot. For one thing, He says plainly, "Lean not unto thine own understanding" (Proverbs 3:5). "Why not?" you ask. Glad you brought that up. When a man leans on his own understanding, he gets deceived into settling for second best, which is the most that common sense can provide. There are better things in store for King's kids who learn how to get at them by using something better than the commonsense approach. Read more about it in *King's Kid* 133; *Victory* 46; *Live the Bible* 57.

Communication gap. See **Language Barrier**

Communion

God's answer: For as often as ye eat this bread, and drink this cup, ye do shew the Lord's death till he come. Wherefore whosoever shall eat this bread, and drink this cup of the Lord, unworthily, shall be guilty of the body and blood of the Lord. But let a man examine himself, and so let him eat of that bread, and drink of that cup. For he that eateth and drinketh unworthily, eateth and drinketh damnation to himself, not discerning the Lord's body. For this cause many are weak and sickly among you, and many sleep. (1 Corinthians 11:26–30)

Comments and mini-report: Receiving Communion or taking the Lord's Supper in the wrong spirit toward others can lead to real trouble. The folks in the Corinthian church had such problems, and Paul said to them and to us, "Many of you are sick and many are dead because of your unforgiveness person to person."

Our body chemistry is designed to reflect the state of the soul, and praying the Lord's Prayer is asking for big trouble—unless we extend to others the forgiveness we are seeking for ourselves.

Our bloodstream was never designed to contain guilt; the only antidote is the blood of Jesus.

Much arthritis, cancer, and other bodily ailments come from buried guilt arising from unforgiveness toward others.

My arthritis refused to yield to much anointing with oil, prayers of exhortation, and fasting. It just got worse until finally I had to do the Bible thing to get healed. Those details you will find in a future King's kid book.

For now you can read other guidelines in *Victory* 200–202.

Complaining. See **Grumbling; Bellyaching**
Computers, King's Kid 66–67, 121

Condemnation (see also **Judging**)
God's answer: There is therefore now no condemnation to them which are in Christ Jesus, who walk not after the flesh, but after the Spirit. (Romans 8:1)

Comments and mini-report: What happens when a King's kid goofs it? Should he feel guilty? Does he lose his salvation?

Shortly after Jesus saved me, I sat in church one Sunday morning with a deep resentment in my heart toward another person. In fact, I was really boiling inside with righteous indignation. That's the kind of indignation you always have when you're blaming someone else for something.

The enemy, Satan, whispered in my ear, "Christians don't think those kinds of thoughts. You're really not saved at all." The feeling of condemnation was scary—and I began to doubt that I was saved after all.

Then the Word of the Lord came to me, "I will never leave you nor forsake you," and from then until now I have flatly refused to receive feelings of condemnation. I know they come from Satan and not from God. You, too, can be free from now on. Read more about condemnation and its origins in *Winner* 185–86; *Victory* 61–64, 111–12, 259.

The other side of condemnation has to do with criticizing and condemning others. It's dangerous business. I've learned—the hard way—that whatever I condemn in others may come to roost on my own doorstep to teach me what I need to know about walking in the other fellow's boots. In *God's in Charge* 40–48 I level with you—for the first time—about one of my own failures. If God hadn't dealt with my pride in a powerful way, I'd be hoping you wouldn't read it. . . .

Confession (see also **Negative Confession**)

God's answer: If we confess our sins, he is faithful and just to forgive us our sins, and to cleanse us from all unrighteousness. (1 John 1:9)

Also I say unto you, Whosoever shall confess me before men, him shall the Son of man also confess before the angels of God. (Luke 12:8)

Confess your faults one to another, and pray one for another, that ye may be healed. (James 5:16)

That if thou shalt confess with thy mouth the Lord Jesus, and shalt believe in thine heart that God hath raised him from the dead, thou shalt be saved. For with the heart man believeth unto righteousness; and with the mouth confession is made unto salvation. (Romans 10:9–10)

Comments and mini-report: Our words have power both to create and to destroy. Right confession brings goodies to God's children; wrong confession brings second-best results to everybody who tries it.

Confessing our faults to one another is scriptural. Our sins are wiped out by the blood of Jesus as we confess them to Him and receive forgiveness. He doesn't even remember them any more.

How do we go about making sure we are making the right kind of confession at all times? Is it possible to stay in a state of "good confession" without falling into the trap of "wrong mouthing"? It surely is not only possible but also highly recommended by God for all King's kids. Read more about confession in *King's Kid* 24, 133–37; *Winner* 68–69; *Victory* 62–63, 198–99.

For a bookful of the benefits of positive confession, read *Live the Bible*—except for chapter 17. You'll just have to forgive me for that episode—but it taught me a lot that I needed to know. It *could* teach you something, too.

Confucianism, King's Kid 19

Contracts
God's answer: Commit thy works unto the Lord, and thy thoughts shall be established. (Proverbs 16:3)

I will instruct thee and teach thee in the way which thou shalt go: I will guide thee with mine eye. (Psalms 32:8)

Delight thyself also in the Lord; and he shall give thee the desires of thine heart. (Psalms 37:4)

Comments and mini-report: How do you get out of a contract—signed in good faith without reading the fine print? Impossible in the natural, especially after you realize there's no way you can perform what's required.

I had gotten into just such a mess and was facing certain disaster for my company and myself—all through my own stupidity. There was no way out except total ruin and loss of everything a lifetime of hard work had produced. My home, car, business, job—and, worst of all, my image as an astute businessman—were at stake.

Could I pray that God would reverse the whole transaction and make it as though it never existed—that it was all a bad dream? Could God do a thing like that?

Until it happened to me, I'd have said, "Forget it, loser, and pay up."

But God did work the miracle for me—and you may need one in your own situation. Try Him!

For further details about the goof that could have cost me everything, read *King's Kid* 133–37. And for another kind of victory over the small print in a contract, try *Victory* 266–68. And for a contract I lost—and got back again better than in the beginning, when I did the Bible thing—read *Live the Bible* 53–57.

Crooked Friends

God's answer: Vengeance is mine; I will repay, saith the Lord. (Romans 12:19b)

But I say unto you, Love your enemies, bless them that curse you, do good to them that hate you, and pray for them which despitefully use you, and persecute you; That ye may be the children of your Father which is in heaven. (Matthew 5:44–45a)

And the Lord turned the captivity of Job, when he prayed for his friends: also the Lord gave Job twice as much as he had before. (Job 42:10)

Comments and mini-report: What does a Christian do when an old and trusted friend refuses to repay a loan made in good faith? Is it okay to take him to court and sue him for your just deserts? Or is that second best?

Rodney, a longtime friend, had borrowed from me a sizable sum to complete his home construction after using up his credit at the bank. Many years later, after he had prospered in our business together, I raised the question about repayment of the loan.

"I'll never pay you! You don't deserve it!" he screamed. "Go ahead and sue me!"

I had his permission, but sensed there was something better in store for me than a court wrangle.

What happened? Read all about it in *Winner* 79–83.

Crowded Conditions

God's answer: Pray without ceasing. (1 Thessalonians 5:17)

But my God shall supply all your need according to his riches in glory by Christ Jesus. (Philippians 4:19)

Comments and mini-report: When the church expansion program is all bogged down under a big mortgage, no more available credit, neighbors who won't sell their property to your group, and a basement that looks more like a swimming pool at high tide, wouldn't it be best just to forget the whole thing?

For some folks, maybe, but not for King's kids. This is the time to see if your heavenly Father can really come through with the "impossible."

Our little church had all the named handicaps—and more. The deacons had prayed and the folks had prayed, but nothing had come of all the prayers, and so all hands were ready to accept defeat—except for three kooky charismatics. They came up with a kooky suggestion: "Why not try a chain of prayer, around-the-clock intercession?"

"That's not Baptist," someone replied.

"Let's try it anyhow," the fanatics countered. "It certainly can't hurt—and it might even help."

"Well, all right," came the grudging permission. "But—"

We tried it. The result? A new education building, new.... But read all about it yourself in *Winner* 159–67. You might find yourself starting a prayer chain, too.

Curtains, Clean, Victory 184–85

Dailey, Starr, King's Kid 85–86
Daniel, Victory 189–91; God's in Charge 28
Daniel's Diet, Flab 61–62
Darwin. See **Evolution vs. Creation**
David and Bathsheba, Winner 63–69; God's in Charge 45
Dead Theology, God's in Charge 32–33
Deafness. See **Hearing Loss**
Death (see also **Graduation Day**), Goo 62–64; God's in Charge 16–17, 81–84, 92, 96

Debts
God's answer: And forgive us our debts, as we forgive our debtors. . . . For if ye forgive men their trespasses, your heavenly Father will also forgive you: But if ye forgive not men their trespasses, neither will your Father forgive your trespasses. (Matthew 6:12, 14–15)

Comments and mini-report: When someone refuses to repay a loan of long standing, and you are dependent on the money to meet a specific obligation, how do you react?

Pagans, of course, resort to process of law and take the debtor to court. The fact that lawyers and other expenses eat up most of the proceeds is beside the point when you have to prove, "He can't *do* that to me!"

How do King's kids handle things like this?

We have the choice of doing it the pagan way and ending up hurting, or trying God's method and having His blessings assured.

Rodney still owes me that large sum of money he borrowed many years ago. But he's the one who hurts!

Read all about it in *Winner* 79–83. And there's more about how to handle unpaid debts in *Victory* 192–204; *God's in Charge* 49–59.

Deceptions. See **Angels of Light; Cayce, Edgar; False Teaching; Fortune Telling; Ouija Boards; Transcendental Meditation**

Deliverance

God's answer: And these signs shall follow them that believe; In my name shall they cast out devils.... (Mark 16:17)

But if I cast out devils by the Spirit of God, then the kingdom of God is come unto you. Or else how can one enter into a strong man's house, and spoil his goods, except he first bind the strong man? and then he will spoil his house. (Matthew 12:28–29)

For the accuser of our brethren is cast down, which accused them before our God day and night. And they overcame him by the blood of the Lamb, and by the word of their testimony. (Revelation 12:10b–11a)

He sent his word, and healed them, and delivered them from their destructions. (Psalms 107:20)

Comments and mini-report: Do all ailments come from evil spirits? No, but some do.

Where does deliverance from demons enter into the healing of bodily ailments?

Some people seem to see a spook behind every sniffle and a demon lurking behind all diseases. Others claim illnesses are their "cross to bear" and at the same time they seek cross-removal through medical means.

Where does each line of thought fit into Bible facts?

When is exorcism valid, and how does it work best?

For some of my experiences with deliverance, read *King's Kid* 189–98; *Winner* 143–49; *Victory* 91–95; *God's in Charge* 81–82.

Demons

God's answer: One cannot rob Satan's kingdom without first binding Satan. Only then can his demons be cast out! (Matthew 12:29 TLB)

And these signs will accompany those who believe; in my name they will cast out demons. (Mark 16:17 RSV)

Comments and mini-report: Are demons active in the world today? Isn't demon possession and all that merely a figure of speech in the Bible? Can't every case be explained psychologically?

A man named Fred asked all those questions as we talked one day about life here and beyond. His training told him, "It's all a state of mind—there are no such things as demons. One day our profession will be able to explain these things in terms of natural phenomena."

It sounded good, and Fred bought it until the day he was at a retreat where a man came with a request for deliverance from a harassing demon.

As we prayed in the Spirit, the gift of discernment operated; the demon was exposed and came out in visible form!

Did Fred see it? Was he convinced?

Read all about it in *King's Kid* 196–97. There's more about demons in *King's Kid* 179–98; *Goo* 53; *Winner* 59–61, 143–49, 180–83; *Victory* 90–95, 196; *God's in Charge* 82.

Depression

God's answer: He healeth the broken in heart, and bindeth up their wounds. (Psalms 147:3)

Humble yourselves in the sight of the Lord, and he shall lift you up. (James 4:10)

For all the promises of God in him are yea, and in him Amen, unto the glory of God by us. (2 Corinthians 1:20)

For whatsoever is born of God overcometh the world: and this is the victory that overcometh the world, even our faith. Who is he that overcometh the world, but he that believeth that Jesus is the Son of God? (1 John 5:4–5)

The Lord also will be a refuge for the oppressed, a refuge in times of trouble. And they that know thy name will put their trust in thee: for thou, Lord, hast not forsaken them that seek thee. (Psalms 9:9–10)

Comments and mini-report: "But everyone gets depressed sometimes," a person commented at a recent workshop on how to live in high victory in Jesus.

"Not me," I reported. "You can leave me out of that mess, because I refuse to get in a state where depression can get control of my feelings."

"How?" they all clamored. "How come you're so smart that you can make such a claim as that?"

"Smart, I am not," I retorted. "I simply do the Bible thing about it—praising God all the time—and I'm never depressed."

To learn how some other folks got rid of their depression, read *Winner* 143–45; *Victory* 197, 250–52.

For how one *didn't* get out of it this side of heaven—yes, that happens sometimes—see *God's in Charge* 82.

Disagreements

God's answer: Therefore if thou bring thy gift to the altar, and there rememberest that thy brother hath ought against thee; Leave there thy gift before the altar, and go thy way; first be reconciled to thy brother, and then come and offer thy gift. (Matthew 5:23–24)

Again I say unto you, That if two of you shall agree on earth as touching any thing that they shall ask, it shall be done for them of my Father which is in heaven. (Matthew 18:19)

And all things are of God, who hath reconciled us to himself by Jesus Christ, and hath given to us the ministry of reconciliation. (2 Corinthians 5:18)

Comments and mini-report: When God directs in a certain way and all sensible signs disagree, shouting, "No way!" who's right? God—or the circumstances? Acting as if God is dependable brings amazing results.

For instance? The Spirit said it was okay for me to rent a car to make the trip from Wiesbaden to Stuttgart that lovely October day in West Germany.

The Hertz rental agent disagreed. "There are no cars available for two weeks," he said. "We're booked solid."

Who was right? The rental agent or God?

Read and find out in *Winner* 121–25. And to see who won in another disagreement, try *Victory* 115–17.

Discerning of Spirits

God's answer: Beloved, believe not every spirit, but try the spirits whether they are of God: because many false prophets are gone out into the world. Hereby know ye the Spirit of God: Every spirit that confesseth that Jesus Christ is come in the flesh is of God: And every spirit that confesseth not that Jesus Christ is come in the flesh is not of God; and this is that spirit of antichrist, whereof ye have heard that it should come; and even now already is it in the world. (1 John 4:1–3)

To another the working of miracles; to another prophecy; to another discerning of spirits.... (1 Corinthians 12:10a)

Comments and mini-report: If one-third of the angels got booted out of heaven for following the wrong leader, awareness of how to deal with them is an important part of King's kid living. Otherwise, the enemy can do his thing in our lives and never get caught at it.

That is why God has given us a gift of the Holy Spirit called "discerning of spirits," so that we can actually "see" with spiritual insight or inner vision exactly what spirit is operating in a given situation.

How does it work? Read more about the discerning of spirits in *King's Kid* 158–65, 193–94; *Winner* 72, 147, 178; *Victory* 95, 259, 285.

Discipline

God's answer: My son, do not make light of the Lord's discipline, and do not lose heart when he rebukes you, because the Lord disciplines those whom he loves, and he punishes everyone he accepts as a son. No discipline seems pleasant at the time, but painful. Later on, however, it produces a harvest of righteousness and peace for those who have been trained by it. (Hebrews 12:5–6, 11 NIV)

Ye have not chosen me, but I have chosen you, and ordained you, that ye should go and bring forth fruit, and that your fruit should remain: that whatsoever ye shall ask of the Father in my name, he may give it you. (John 15:16)

Those whom I love I rebuke and discipline. (Revelation 3:19a NIV)

Comments and mini-report: "My salvation makes me free from the laws of God, so I no longer need discipline," remarked a well-meaning but misinformed new King's kid who had no awareness of the need for further training. He couldn't have been more wrong.

Why is discipline necessary for King's kids? Why, for our own progress in spiritual growth and maturity as well as to assure us of God's best in this life and beyond.

Rebellion is standard equipment in the human mechanism. For victorious living, rebellion needs to be replaced by submission to the Spirit of God. How does all that work? Come to the vineyard and have a look in *Victory* 131–35.

Discouragement (see also **Depression**)
God's answer: For he hath said, I will never leave thee, nor forsake thee. (Hebrews 13:5b)

Nay, in all these things we are more than conquerors through him that loved us. (Romans 8:37)

Being confident of this very thing, that he which hath begun a good work in you will perform it until the day of Jesus Christ. (Philippians 1:6)

Don't be frightened by the size of the task, for the Lord my God is with you; he will not forsake you. He will see to it that everything is finished correctly. (1 Chronicles 28:20b TLB)

Take courage, my soul! Do you remember those times (but how could you ever forget them!) when you led a great procession to the Temple on festival days, singing with joy, praising the Lord? Why then be downcast? Why be discouraged and sad? Hope in God! I shall yet praise him again. Yes, I shall again praise him for his help. (Psalms 42:4–5 TLB)

And let us not get tired of doing what is right, for after a while we will reap a harvest of blessing if we don't get discouraged and give up. (Galatians 6:9 TLB)

Comments and mini-report: The only kind of Christian the Lord cannot use is the discouraged one. An attitude of defeat produces a do-nothingness that leads to utter hopelessness.

Is it possible to live above the level of such an abyss? Yes. But how can we function without being discouraged when the world is in such a state of chaos?

Some of what I have learned about these things is reported in *Winner* xvii–xviii; *Victory* 30, 227–30.

Disintegrated spinal disk. See **Back Trouble**
Disobedience. See **Rebellion**

Dispensationalism

God's answer: Verily, verily, I say unto you, He that believeth on me, the works that I do shall he do also; and greater works than these shall he do; because I go unto my Father. (John 14:12)

Jesus Christ the same yesterday, and to day, and for ever. (Hebrews 13:8)

Comments and mini-report: Have you ever been told about any of God's promises, "That's not for today"?

That's called dispensationalism—dispensing with the things of God no longer popular among the doctrines of men. Dispensationalism happens to be a particular hang-up with my denomination, which happens to be Southern Baptist. We're specialists in dispensing with the things we've decided God is no longer any good at—healing, for instance.

I am happy to report that God is still in the healing business. How do I know? Glad you asked. I know because I got a brand-new spinal disk while I waited. He dispensed with the old one and gave me one that didn't hurt. Read all about it in *King's Kid* 39–43. And there's more about dispensationalism in *Winner* 102–6; *Victory* 99–103.

Divorce

God's answer: But I tell you that anyone who divorces his wife, except for marital unfaithfulness, causes her to commit adultery, and anyone who marries a woman so divorced commits adultery. (Matthew 5:32 NIV)

Comments and mini-report: Divorce is a subject on which I used to be holier than thou. For how I learned not to look down my shiny nose at persons who had gone through the agony of divorce, read *God's in Charge* 40–48.

Doctrines, Man-Made, God's in Charge 121–27, 138

Doers of the Word
God's answer: For if any be a hearer of the word, and not a doer, he is like unto a man beholding his natural face in a glass: For he beholdeth himself, and goeth his way, and straightway forgetteth what manner of man he was. But whoso looketh into the perfect law of liberty, and continueth therein, he being not a forgetful hearer, but a doer of the work, this man shall be blessed in his deed. (James 1:23–25)

The Kingdom of God is not just talking; it is living by God's power. (1 Corinthians 4:20 TLB)

Yes, but even more blessed are all who hear the Word of God and put it into practice. (Luke 11:28 TLB)

Comments and mini-report: "But if I understood the Bible, then I would do it and get results," the human mind likes to argue.

God doesn't have much to say about our understanding His Word. "My thoughts are above your thoughts," He tells us. But He does have a lot to say about our being doers of the Word. As a matter of fact, He highly recommends it.

How do you go about being a doer of any teaching? Not by thinking about it or arguing about what it means. You simply read it and act as if it's true by doing it and expecting things to happen.

Do you want a solid foundation under you at all times? Is there really a place of absolute assurance, regardless of appearances?

There surely is—for doers of the Word. There's

more about how you can go about being a doer of the Word in *King's Kid* 102–5, 116–17; *Winner* 87–92; *Victory* 11–23, 96–98, 219–21, 238–39; *Goo* 89; and, of course, in *Live the Bible,* from the beginning to the end. (Well, chapter 17 is more like "how *not* to live it.")

Dogs, Training of, Victory 265

Doing God's Will
God's answer: Rejoice evermore. Pray without ceasing. In every thing give thanks: for this is the will of God in Christ Jesus concerning you. (1 Thessalonians 5:16–18)

And be not conformed to this world: but be ye transformed by the renewing of your mind, that ye may prove what is that good, and acceptable, and perfect, will of God. (Romans 12:2)

Comments and mini-report: Right after I became a King's kid by receiving Jesus into my heart, I got to thinking along these lines: "If only I could know God's perfect will for me at all times, by His grace I would do it and be happy continually."

My prayer was based on His promise in the Word. (See *God's answer* above.)

"Lord," I prayed, "show me how I can be in the center of Your will at all times so I'll never be in doubt for one instant the rest of my life."

And the Lord did show me, and from then until this moment, I've been in the exact middle of His will—regardless of feelings, appearances, and symptoms to the contrary.

How do I manage all that? Read about it in *Victory* 68–74, 299–300. For further adventures in doing

God's will—which is the same as being a doer of His Word—read *Flab* 37–43; *Live the Bible*—all of it (except for chapter 17).

Doublemindedness. See **Single-mindedness**
Downing, Frank, King's Kid 143

Drinking Too Much
God's answer: He himself gives life and breath to everything and satisfies every need there is. (Acts 17:25b TLB)

My grace is sufficient for thee: for my strength is made perfect in weakness. (2 Corinthians 12:9a)

All things are lawful unto me, but all things are not expedient: all things are lawful for me, but I will not be brought under the power of any. (1 Corinthians 6:12)

And be not drunk with wine, wherein is excess; but be filled with the Spirit. (Ephesians 5:18)

Comments and mini-report: When is drinking too much a danger signal? Is the person who drinks too much an alcoholic? Isn't it all a matter of willpower?

All these questions are being asked every hour about a loved one or friend who "drinks too much."

Who are the alcoholics as opposed to those who "drink too much"? Those bums in other people's lives are the alcoholics, of course! Your own kinfolk *couldn't* be that bad—or could they?

Do you really want to help someone who drinks too much? Even if it's you? These King's kid reports may help: *King's Kid* 11–16; *Winner* 191–93; *Victory* 1–10, 12–14; *God's in Charge* 21–30, 119.

Educated Idiots and the Educated Idiot Box

God's answer: For God says, "I will destroy all human plans of salvation no matter how wise they seem to be, and ignore the best ideas of men, even the most brilliant of them." So what about these wise men, these scholars, these brilliant debaters of this world's great affairs? God has made them all look foolish, and shown their wisdom to be useless nonsense. For God in his wisdom saw to it that the world would never find God through human brilliance, and then he stepped in and saved all those who believed his message, which the world calls foolish and silly. (1 Corinthians 1:19–21 TLB)

Verily I say unto you, Except ye be converted, and become as little children, ye shall not enter into the kingdom of heaven. (Matthew 18:3)

But God hath chosen the foolish things of the world to confound the wise; and God hath chosen the weak things of the world to confound the things which are mighty; And base things of the world, and things which are despised, hath God chosen, yea, and things which are not, to bring to nought things that are: That no flesh should glory in his presence. (1 Corinthians 1:27–29)

Stop fooling yourselves. If you count yourself above average in intelligence, as judged by this world's standards, you had better put this all aside and be a fool rather than let it hold you back from the true wisdom from above. For the wisdom of this world is foolishness to God. As it says in the book of Job, God uses man's own brilliance to trap him; he stumbles over his own "wisdom" and falls. And again, in the book of Psalms, we are told that the Lord knows full well how the human mind reasons, and how foolish and futile it is. (1 Corinthians 3:18–20 TLB)

Comments and mini-report: Up to the point where I became a King's kid by asking Jesus to move in and take over, my life had been spent exclusively in the world of scientific things. It was natural that I would see everything in that light. After I was saved, however, the Holy Spirit opened up my understanding in the light of His Word, and I realized that with all my education and training, I was simply an educated idiot.

The product of three of our great learning institutions but with no awareness of God in human affairs—that *has* to be the ultimate in stupidity! And so I was. My teachers had taught me well how to *make* a living, but nothing at all about how to *live* life successfully on planet earth. I learned all that without going back to school, by learning to live the Bible in my everyday affairs.

How did we get to be educated idiots in the first place? You can read all about these things in *King's Kid* xi, 6–7, 181–82; *Goo* 67; *Winner* 31, 102; *Victory* 41, 105, 240–49; *Live the Bible* 32–33; *God's in Charge* 69, 137.

Ego Trips
God's answer: Let nothing be done through strife or vainglory; but in lowliness of mind let each esteem

other better than themselves. Look not every man on his own things, but every man also on the things of others. (Philippians 2:3–4)

But he that is greatest among you shall be your servant. And whosoever shall exalt himself shall be abased; and he that shall humble himself shall be exalted. (Matthew 23:11–12)

But he that glorieth, let him glory in the Lord. For not he that commendeth himself is approved, but whom the Lord commendeth. (2 Corinthians 10:17–18)

He that speaketh of himself seeketh his own glory: but he that seeketh his glory that sent him, the same is true, and no unrighteousness is in him. (John 7:18)

The Lord says: Let not the wise man bask in his wisdom, nor the mighty man in his might, nor the rich man in his riches. Let them boast in this alone: That they truly know me, and understand that I am the Lord of justice and of righteousness whose love is steadfast; and that I love to be this way. (Jeremiah 9:23–24 TLB)

Comments and mini-report: Why does ego-tripping self-effort produce frustration in the end? What's wrong with insisting on my rights to myself, getting my own way, and being happy?

Maybe nothing's wrong with it, but it doesn't produce the desired results. In fact, it just plain doesn't work.

I tried my own way for the first forty-eight years of my life and got more and more miserable. Then I met Jesus and He tuned me in to a whole new basis for living—submitting my rights to myself into His hands. It didn't make any sense at all for me to give up my rights to myself—but strangely enough, it really worked.

For instance? Read the account in *Victory* 11–17; *God's in Charge* 15–17.

Egyptians, Victory 49–50
Einstein, Goo 20–22; Victory 36–37
Elijah, Victory 154–55; Live the Bible 22

Emptiness

God's answer: My heart and my flesh crieth out for the living God. (Psalms 84:2b)

And ye are complete in him, which is the head of all principality and power. (Colossians 2:10)

I am come that they might have life, and that they might have it more abundantly. (John 10:10b)

And ye shall seek me, and find me, when ye shall search for me with all your heart. (Jeremiah 29:13)

Look! I have been standing at the door and I am constantly knocking. If anyone hears me calling him and opens the door, I will come in and fellowship with him and he with me. (Revelation 3:20 TLB)

And to know the love of Christ, which passeth knowledge, that ye might be filled with all the fulness of God. (Ephesians 3:19)

Yes, everything else is worthless when compared with the priceless gain of knowing Christ Jesus my Lord. I have put aside all else, counting it worth less than nothing, in order that I can have Christ. (Philippians 3:8–9 TLB)

71

Comments and mini-report: Emptiness. It can happen when your calendar is jam-packed with Important Activities and Indispensable Appointments, when your life seems—to outsiders—running over with meaning. But down inside, where you really live, there's an aching void bigger than all outdoors. And you know that in reality, your life is as empty as the bottom half of this page.

The remedy for that awful emptiness? Jesus, the One who fills all things. Read all about it in *King's Kid* 9–12, 16–17, 73–74; *Goo* 66; *Winner* 12–14, 74–77; *Victory* 76–78, 217–221; *God's in Charge* 22–24.

Eternal life. See **Born Again, How to Be**
Eve. See **Adam and Eve**

Evolution vs. Creation

God's answer: And God created great whales, and
every living creature that moveth, which the waters
brought forth abundantly, after their kind, and every
winged fowl after his kind: and God saw that it was
good. And God said, Let the earth bring forth the living creature after his kind, cattle, and creeping thing,
and beast of the earth after his kind: and it was so.
And God said, Let us make man in our image, after
our likeness. (Genesis 1:21, 24, 26a)

All flesh is not the same flesh: but there is one kind of
flesh of men, another flesh of beasts, another of fishes,
and another of birds. (1 Corinthians 15:39)

In the beginning was the Word, and the Word was
with God, and the Word was God. The same was in
the beginning with God. All things were made by
him; and without him was not any thing made that
was made. (John 1:1–3)

Comments and mini-report: How did you get here? By
a series of accidents, as evolutionists would lead you
to believe, or by the special creative act of a loving
heavenly Father who created you in His image?

For many years, this question was of no real concern to me. Then I realized that evolution was being
taught in our schools as fact, while our children were
being prohibited from hearing about the possibility of
a creator God who made all that is.

Are you in doubt as to how it all began? Do you
wonder what really happened? How can you give cor-

rect answers to your children when they ask about
these things?

Simple. Read all of *How Did It All Begin?* (*From
Goo to You by Way of the Zoo*); *King's Kid* 20.

Exercise, Flab 79–83
Exorcism. See **Demons**

Eyeball Ailments
God's answer: Heal me, O Lord, and I shall be healed;
save me, and I shall be saved: for thou art my praise.
(Jeremiah 17:14)

The Lord will perfect that which concerneth me: thy
mercy, O Lord, endureth for ever. (Psalms 138:8a)

The Spirit of the Lord is upon me, because he hath
anointed me to preach the gospel to the poor; he hath
sent me to heal the brokenhearted, to preach deliverance to the captives, and recovering of sight to the
blind, to set at liberty them that are bruised. (Luke
4:18)

Comments and mini-report: When total blindness in
one eye results from an accident, should you accept it
as being needed within the scope of your spiritual life?
Or should it be considered of satanic origin?

When a laser beam disintegrated the retina of my
left eye, my friends assured me that the enemy was at
work in my life. My first reaction was to agree with
them and to organize a gigantic pity party complete
with twenty-nine different flavors of martyr pills.

Then the Word of the Lord came to my deliverance
and I began to do the Bible thing about it—and to
keep on doing it. The result? Well, it's too soon for the
final result, but you can read the interim report in

Victory 109–11. For other accounts of how God works in the midst of eyeball ailments, try *Victory* 107–9, 115–17; *Live the Bible* 41–42; *God's in Charge* 28–29, 71–80, 126.

Eyeball Guidance

God's answer: I will instruct thee and teach thee in the way which thou shalt go: I will guide thee with mine eye. (Psalms 32:8)

Comments and mini-report: "I will guide thee with mine eye," God says. When I came across that Scripture awhile ago, I asked myself a couple of questions: "What does it mean to be guided by the eye of God? Can I see Him eye to eye?"

When my Educated Idiot Box didn't come up with any satisfactory answers, I asked the Lord about these things, then added, "Lord, if I can be led by You constantly and directly, as an eyeball-to-eyeball relationship suggests, I sure want it."

I still didn't know how to get into that position until the Holy Spirit began to teach me through the Word of God and through things He brought to my mind about fancy table settings and the ways of hunting dogs. Strange combination, you think? Well, His ways are above our ways.

Anyhow, shortly after my request reached heaven, I was watching the field trials of some retrievers. Their undivided attention on their trainers caught my eye, and the Lord began to teach me along these lines: When our attention is exclusively on the things of God, with nothing in between, and our hearts are right with Jesus, our Savior, eyeball-to-eyeball guidance *is* ours if we know how to act like it.

How? Read *Victory* 263–65.

Faith

God's answer: Now faith is the substance of things hoped for, the evidence of things not seen. (Hebrews 11:1)

For whatsoever is born of God overcometh the world: and this is the victory that overcometh the world, even our faith. (1 John 5:4)

So then faith cometh by hearing, and hearing by the word of God. (Romans 10:17)

And Jesus said unto them, Because of your unbelief: for verily I say unto you, If ye have faith as a grain of mustard seed, ye shall say unto this mountain, Remove hence to yonder place; and it shall remove; and nothing shall be impossible unto you. (Matthew 17:20)

God hath dealt to every man the measure of faith. (Romans 12:3b)

Comments and mini-report: Faith comes in two packages: faith in God and His Word and faith in the evidence of our senses.

Jesus' words, "Have faith in God," contain the clue to victorious living during our stay on planet earth. But how is this possible in this world of crime, violence, unbelief, and growing pollution? The answer is so simple it eludes all but those who are King's kids all the way.

For more about faith and what it can do, read *King's Kid* 101–2, 191–92; *Winner* 102–3; *Victory* 25–39, 112–14, 234–35; *God's in Charge* 81, 92–93.

False Teaching

God's answer: Now the Spirit speaketh expressly, that in the latter times some shall depart from the faith, giving heed to seducing spirits, and doctrines of devils. (1 Timothy 4:1)

That we henceforth be no more children, tossed to and fro, and carried about with every wind of doctrine, by the sleight of men, and cunning craftiness, whereby they lie in wait to deceive; But speaking the truth in love, may grow up into him in all things, which is the head, even Christ. (Ephesians 4:14–15)

Beloved, believe not every spirit, but try the spirits whether they are of God: because many false prophets are gone out into the world. Hereby know ye the Spirit of God: Every spirit that confesseth that Jesus Christ is come in the flesh is of God: And every spirit that confesseth not that Jesus Christ is come in the flesh is not of God; and this is that spirit of antichrist, whereof ye have heard that it should come; and even now already is it in the world. (1 John 4:1–3)

O foolish Galatians, who hath bewitched you, that ye should not obey the truth, before whose eyes Jesus Christ hath been evidently set forth, crucified among you? (Galatians 3:1)

Comments and mini-report: How can you tell the difference between Truth and error when confronted by the scores of religious movements active all around us?

Can a King's kid be protected against the false teaching of cults without running the risk of rejecting Truth along with falsehood?

It happens that I was involved in just about every false cult imaginable before I met Jesus Christ as the true Way to the Father. These experiences can only be considered valuable tools now that my eyes have been opened to the Truth through God's Word.

In my King's kid reports I share with you many of the typical error symptoms and how to detect the most glaring of them.

Of course, without the gifts of the Holy Spirit, it is still possible to fall into error. In fact, many spiritual leaders have done just that.

How can you be assured it won't happen to you? Read my reports and pray! The reports? Try *King's Kid* 19–21; *Winner* 178; *Victory* 281–300; *God's in Charge* 82–84; and the reports listed under **Cayce, Edgar; Christian Science; Evolution vs. Creation; Jehovah's Witnesses; Transcendental Meditation; Unity;** and **Universalism.**

Family, Salvation of

God's answer: Likewise, ye wives, be in subjection to your own husbands; that, if any obey not the word, they also may without the word be won by the conversation of the wives; While they behold your chaste conversation coupled with fear. (1 Peter 3:1–2)

Believe on the Lord Jesus Christ, and thou shalt be saved, and thy house. (Acts 16:31)

Comments and mini-report: Do you have unsaved loved ones? Most King's kids do. Are you praying for them daily? Most King's kids do that, too, but not the ones who know how these things really work. Stop praying and do the Bible thing and you'll begin to see things happen.

How do I know? It happened in my own experience.

After I got saved, I began working on my wife and teenage daughter. I tried every wrong approach in the book. The harder I tried, the further away they got, until I became so obnoxious our household was a total mess.

Then I did the Bible thing about it and they both got saved in six weeks!

Try the Bible method on your loved ones. What is the Bible method? Glad you asked. For details, read *King's Kid* 150–51; *Victory* 179–80.

Fasting, Flab 2, 36, 139–40
Fat. See **Flabbitis**
Faultfinding. See **Grumbling**

Fear

God's answer: For God hath not given us the spirit of fear; but of power, and of love, and of a sound mind. (2 Timothy 1:7)

I sought the Lord, and he heard me, and delivered me from all my fears. (Psalms 34:4)

Fear thou not; for I am with thee: be not dismayed; for I am thy God: I will strengthen thee; yea, I will help thee; yea, I will uphold thee with the right hand of my righteousness. (Isaiah 41:10)

The fear of man bringeth a snare: but whoso putteth his trust in the Lord shall be safe. (Proverbs 29:25)

And the Lord, he it is that doth go before thee; he will be with thee, he will not fail thee, neither forsake thee: fear not, neither be dismayed. (Deuteronomy 31:8)

There is no fear in love; but perfect love casteth out fear: because fear hath torment. He that feareth is not made perfect in love. (1 John 4:18)

Comments and mini-report: Fear comes in two varieties. One is faith in failure, the other is the result of demonic activity.

Perfect faith in failure brought Job all the things he expected: total disaster. And faith in failure used to bring me the same results, until I learned better ways to handle adversity.

The fear that comes from demonic activity can be dealt with directly—the Bible way. So can the fear that comes from faith in failure.

How does it work? Read on. You'll find King's kid reports on these things in *King's Kid* 185–87; *Goo* 76; *Winner* vii; *Victory* 222–24, 253–54.

Feelings

God's answer: Judge not according to the appearance, but judge righteous judgment. (John 7:24)

Do ye look on things after the outward appearance? If any man trust to himself that he is Christ's, let him of himself think this again, that, as he is Christ's, even so are we Christ's. (2 Corinthians 10:7)

For we walk by faith, not by sight. (2 Corinthians 5:7)

Comments and mini-report: When are feelings reliable as an indicator of things spiritual? Almost never.

Feelings are rooted in the soul, the human part of us, and are influenced by happenings which change moment by moment.

All five of our senses are constantly transmitting data to our heads, where positive or negative decisions are made, generally based on trouble-borrowing tactics like these:

"Suppose such and such a thing happens and I have to take thus and such an action?"

"How do I know what worse thing will surely happen tomorrow?"

I used to be an expert at "supposing" and borrowing trouble from the future. Then I learned how to take hold of the Truth the Bible talks about. You can learn it, too. Pick up some pointers in *Winner* 15, 21, 130; *Victory* 25–30, 73, 151, 155–56, 184–87.

Firebombs

God's answer: The fear of man bringeth a snare: but whoso putteth his trust in the Lord shall be safe. (Proverbs 29:25)

Fear ye not, stand still, and see the salvation of the Lord, which he will shew to you to day. (Exodus 14:13a)

Comments and mini-report: The rioters had sent word, "If you gather in that restaurant tonight, we will burn your meeting to the ground—with you in it!" We knew it was no idle chatter; they meant business. Buildings all around us were already in flames as the city of Albuquerque was taken over by the mobs.

We had a choice that night of running away or "having done all, to stand and see the salvation of the Lord in the land of the living," as the Word says. Which would it be?

Do King's kids have to run like dogs for fear of the threats of the enemy? Is it "tempting God," as one person commented, to stay and "face the music"?

Is our God personally interested in this sort of thing? Would He really intervene in the midst of pagan rioters? We decided to find out.

The answers He gave us that night were reassuring for all time. Our God is *able!*

For further details, read *King's Kid* 117–20.

Flattened Billfold

God's answer: And on the morrow when he departed, he took out two pence, and gave them to the host, and said unto him, Take care of him; and whatsoever thou spendest more, when I come again, I will repay thee. (Luke 10:35)

Comments and mini-report: A flat billfold is never a problem for King's kids because we have a rich heavenly Father. The "other kind" have to worry about these things!

When the midnight phone call turns out to be a fellow human being requiring help, and upon arrival you find he needs medical help *fast* and you're low on funds, what do you do?

If you're caught in an ownership position, you hesitate just long enough to hit the panic button and then make excuses for leaving him to "do the best he can," which is probably to die in misery. But if you're a steward—

I've been in that predicament, where the person was in the throes of alcoholic convulsions and would probably not live through the night without help. What happened?

I can report that I have never known a case—imaginary or real—where God did not intervene with an abundant supply "beyond anything I could imagine!"

For fuller details, read *Victory* 11–17.

Fleeces

God's answer: And he said unto him, If now I have found grace in thy sight, then shew me a sign that thou talkest with me. (Judges 6:17)

Behold, I will put a fleece of wool in the floor; and if the dew be on the fleece only, and it be dry upon all the earth beside, then shall I know that thou wilt save Israel by mine hand, as thou hast said. (Judges 6:37)

Comments and mini-report: When are fleeces acceptable to God and when are they the sign of unbelief? Good questions, and ones frequently heard at meetings of King's kids.

One dear old saint was heard to remark, "The use of fleeces is entirely juvenile and indicates a lack of maturity in the spiritual life."

She will have to call me junior.

Are you bothered by questions and doubts about fleeces? Do I personally ever depend on fleeces for guidance after walking in the Spirit for about thirty years now?

Read all about it in King's kid reports in *King's Kid* 206; *Winner* 113–14; *Victory* 167–72.

Flip-Your-Flab-Forever Program, Flab 45–50

Fog

God's answer: For now we see through a glass, darkly; but then face to face: now I know in part; but then shall I know even as also I am known. (1 Corinthians 13:12)

For we walk by faith, not by sight. (2 Corinthians 5:7)

Comments and mini-report: What's the best thing to do when the fog is too thick for a duck to take off safely? Is it better to cancel the trip until better weather, or is it safe to trust Jesus for something supernatural to set in?

The day I left Washington, D.C., for Greenville, South Carolina, to speak at some meetings, I had that decision to make. In fact, the plane was already hours late as I called the brother to say I was on my way and would arrive when Jesus got me there!

Landing in Charlotte, North Carolina, I found the major airlines all solidly grounded, but there was a lone one-man shuttle service who would attempt the trip—without guaranteeing *anything* except uncertainty. It was the best deal I could find under the circumstances, so while common sense hollered, "Forget it!" this King's kid said, "Let's go! What are we waiting for?"

What happened? Lots of things detrimental to the kingdom of darkness. Afterward, I had to agree that Slue Foot certainly had good reason for not wanting me in Greenville that night!

Read all about it in *King's Kid* 139–42.

Food Cravings, Flab 27–43
Food for the soul. See **Soul Food**
Food for the spirit. See **Spiritual Food**
Footnote Theology, Victory 90–98

Forgiveness (see also **Unforgiveness**)
God's answer: So overflowing is his kindness towards us that he took away all our sins through the blood of his Son, by whom we are saved. (Ephesians 1:7 TLB)

But if we walk in the light, as he is in the light, we have fellowship one with another, and the blood of Jesus Christ his Son cleanseth us from all sin. (1 John 1:7)

In fact we can say that under the old agreement almost everything was cleansed by sprinkling it with blood, and without the shedding of blood there is no forgiveness of sins. (Hebrews 9:22 TLB)

Having therefore, brethren, boldness to enter into the holiest by the blood of Jesus. (Hebrews 10:19)

Comments and mini-report: I had no idea of the deep-seated effects of guilt in the lives of King's kids until the Lord began to teach me about it in His Word. David the king was a prime example of a man who was about to come apart at the seams from buried guilt until he confessed his sin and received God's forgiveness.

That perfect forgiveness was administered to me about thirty years ago when I became a King's kid in training. I still need a dose of it occasionally when I exercise my right to goof everything I touch. To learn how David got forgiveness, how I got some, and how you can get it for yourself, read *King's Kid* 17–18, 24, 199–213; *Winner* 66–69; *God's in Charge* 45.

Fortune-Telling, King's Kid 20
Fossils, Goo 27–49

Fouled-Up Flight Plans
God's answer: And we know that all things work together for good to them that love God, to them who are the called according to his purpose. (Romans 8:28)

Comments and mini-report: The flight schedule prepared for me by my heretofore reliable travel agent called for changing to a flight which turned out to be nonexistent.

"When I get home I'll fire that stupid agent!" I fumed, and my anger doubled when I learned that the next flight was many hours in the future.

Then the Holy Spirit came to my rescue, reminding me how a King's kid ought to act to get best results. After the timely reminder, I wrapped the whole mess up in praise and turned it over to Jesus for further instructions.

What happened? A healing service right there in the big new airport at Jacksonville, Florida. It couldn't have happened if the travel agent hadn't arranged a "wrong" schedule, proving again that there are no mistakes in the lives of King's kids. There were other blessings, too, which only a loving God could bring about as a King's kid dared to get on His wavelength by praising Him in spite of appearances. In fact, things got so good, I almost missed my connection to an existent flight several hours later!

Read all about it in *Winner* 151–57, and for further incidents in which God got the glory in the midst of flight snafus, see *King's Kid* 1–6, 139–42.

Fractured Marriage, God's in Charge 34–48, 130–32

Fruit-Bearing
God's answer: And the cares of this world, and the deceitfulness of riches, and the lusts of other things entering in, choke the word, and it becometh unfruitful. (Mark 4:19)

But his delight is in the law of the Lord; and in his law doth he meditate day and night. And he shall be like a tree planted by the rivers of water, that bringeth forth his fruit in his season; his leaf also shall not wither; and whatsoever he doeth shall prosper. (Psalms 1:2–3)

Abide in me, and I in you. As the branch cannot bear fruit of itself, except it abide in the vine; no more can ye, except ye abide in me. (John 15:4)

Ye have not chosen me, but I have chosen you, and ordained you, that ye should go and bring forth fruit, and that your fruit should remain: that whatsoever ye shall ask of the Father in my name, he may give it you. (John 15:16)

Comments and mini-report: Ask a dozen King's kids, "What is the fruit of a Christian?" and you'll likely get a dozen wrong answers.

Based on simple seed-to-fruit principles, the fruit of a Christian is baby Christians, of course. And the fruit of the Spirit in the life of a Christian is so plainly listed in Galatians 5:23 that most King's kids know about that.

But how does one become a fruit-bearer? First, he has to come under the control of the heavenly Vine-dresser. That *could* mean painful pruning of second best. Are you ready?

Some of the principles of fruit-bearing and how they work are detailed in *Victory* 121–35; *God's in Charge* 105–120.

Frustration

God's answer: Now thanks be unto God, which always causeth us to triumph in Christ. (2 Corinthians 2:14a)

I can do all things through Christ which strengtheneth me. (Philippians 4:13)

My grace is sufficient for thee: for my strength is made perfect in weakness. Most gladly therefore will I rather glory in my infirmities, that the power of Christ may rest upon me. (2 Corinthians 12:9)

Greater is he that is in you, than he that is in the world. (1 John 4:4b)

Comments and mini-report: What causes frustration? Ignorance of God's method of working out the details of His perfect will in our lives.

As a new Christian I was told, "Ask God to help you run your life."

That sounded real good, and it worked—for a while. But then God closed His ears more and more to my foolish prayers.

"Foolish?" you ask.

Yes, foolish. Because there's a much better way to handle life, and I found out how.

For details, see *Goo* 86; *Victory* 42; *Flab* 31–36.

Fullness of Time

God's answer: But when the fulness of the time was come, God sent forth his Son, made of a woman, made under the law. (Galatians 4:4)

That in the dispensation of the fulness of times he might gather together in one all things in Christ, both which are in heaven, and which are on earth; even in him. (Ephesians 1:10)

Comments and mini-report: Until I learned that God works in a time frame called "the fullness of time," I was in constant state of uncertainty about my prayer life.

Had I prayed amiss?

Was I out of God's grace?

Had I neglected to recognize and confess some hidden sin?

I simply did not understand that God's ways are different from our ways and that He sometimes has many details to arrange before we can handle the answer He is sending.

Understanding the principle of "the fullness of time" took me awhile, but when I caught on, I was relieved of a bundle of anxiety. You will be, too.

Read more about God's timetable in *Victory* 110, 127; *Live the Bible* 18–19; *God's in Charge* 26–33, 71–79, 159.

Furry Things, King's Kid 196–97

Gambling

God's answer: Set your affection on things above, not on things on the earth. (Colossians 3:2)

And have no fellowship with the unfruitful works of darkness, but rather reprove them. (Ephesians 5:11)

All things are lawful for me, but all things are not expedient: all things are lawful for me, but all things edify not. (1 Corinthians 10:23)

For a man is a slave to whatever controls him. (2 Peter 2:19b TLB)

Comments and mini-report: "But a little wager now and then between friends never hurt anyone," Charlie insisted. Two weeks later, he watched, bewildered, as the loan company trucked away the last of his furniture and appliances.

Did you ever try to stop doing a no-no?

I did. When I met Jesus, I was a compulsive cardplayer. After becoming aware of certain Scriptures about such things, I tried to quit.

Naturally, I got worse and worse. Then Jesus came to my rescue.

Read all about it in *King's Kid* 27–29.

Gifts of the Holy Spirit

God's answer: Verily, verily, I say unto you, He that believeth on me, the works that I do shall he do also; and greater works than these shall he do; because I go unto my Father. (John 14:12)

Every good gift and every perfect gift is from above, and cometh down from the Father of lights, with whom is no variableness, neither shadow of turning. (James 1:17)

For God's gifts and his call can never be withdrawn; he will never go back on his promises. (Romans 11:29 TLB)

Now you have every grace and blessing; every spiritual gift and power for doing his will are yours during this time of waiting for the return of our Lord Jesus Christ. (1 Corinthians 1:7 TLB)

Now there are diversities of gifts, but the same Spirit. (1 Corinthians 12:4)

Comments and mini-report: Are all the gifts of the Holy Spirit operating in the Church today?

Who gets which gift?

90

Does every Christian get at least one gift? If so, how can you be sure which one is for you?

Bone up on the gifts of the Holy Spirit in *King's Kid* 104–5; *Winner* 184; *Victory* 231–40, 269–75; *God's in Charge* 112–13, 158–59.

GIGO, Live the Bible 20–21
Girdles, Flab 13–16
Glory meter. See **Liebman's Glory Meter**
Gluttony Trail, Flab 12
God's will. See **Doing God's Will**
Golbeck, Kay, Live the Bible 120–21
Good for nothing. See **Unworthiness**

Good Works (see also **Programitis**)
God's answer: And then there is your "righteousness" and your "good works"—none of which will save you. (Isaiah 57:12 TLB)

Not by works of righteousness which we have done, but according to his mercy he saved us, by the washing of regeneration, and renewing of the Holy Ghost. (Titus 3:5)

For by grace are ye saved through faith; and that not of yourselves: it is the gift of God: Not of works, lest any man should boast. (Ephesians 2:8–9)

But we are all as an unclean thing, and all our righteousnesses are as filthy rags. (Isaiah 64:6a)

Comments and mini-report: Are you a Brownie-point Christian?

Are you good enough to stay saved?

Were you good enough to get saved in the first place? If so, you're in bad shape.

That's the way my friend Ed told it to me about thirty years ago when he introduced me to Jesus.

But that's not all. He went on to say that I could do anything I liked after I met Jesus.

Try it! And discover, as I did, that Jesus will take some things away when we get tired of second best and tell Him so.

More details in *King's Kid* 24; *Victory* 80, 295.

Gossip

God's answer: If any man among you seem to be religious, and bridleth not his tongue, but deceiveth his own heart, this man's religion is vain. (James 1:26)

Only let your conversation be as it becometh the gospel of Christ. (Philippians 1:27a)

The words of a talebearer are as wounds, and they go down into the innermost parts of the belly. (Proverbs 18:8)

Comments and mini-report: "Now, I don't mean to gossip, but. . . ."

Sound familiar?

"But someone has to tell it, and it might as well be me," you alibi, and your ulcers burn more brightly!

Your colitis does likewise, and your intestinal "flu" flies higher!

Just how does the wrong use of the mouth result in these internal disorders?

You didn't know that "tongue trouble" causes many such ailments? Neither did I, until. . . .

Read all about it in *King's Kid* 81–87, 195.

Graduation Day

God's answer: Jesus said unto her, I am the resurrection, and the life: he that believeth in me, though he were dead, yet shall he live: And whosoever liveth and believeth in me shall never die. (John 11:25–26)

Death is swallowed up in victory.... But thanks be to God, which giveth us the victory through our Lord Jesus Christ. (1 Corinthians 15:54b, 57)

Therefore we are always confident, knowing that, whilst we are at home in the body, we are absent from the Lord: (For we walk by faith, not by sight:) We are confident, I say, and willing rather to be absent from the body, and to be present with the Lord. (2 Corinthians 5:6–8)

Yea, though I walk through the valley of the shadow of death, I will fear no evil: for thou art with me. (Psalms 23:4a)

Verily, verily, I say unto you, If a man keep my saying, he shall never see death. (John 8:51)

For this purpose the Son of God was manifested, that he might destroy the works of the devil. (1 John 3:8b)

Comments and mini-report: When a King's kid leaves this life for the new dimension of eternity, it's really a graduation exercise in God's sight.

"He that believeth in me shall never die," is the assurance Jesus gives us.

When I was at the point of death, all this became very real to me. Read all about it in *Winner* 189–91. And for further graduation exercises, see *King's Kid* 121–22, 147–49; *Victory* 157–58, 191.

93

Grapevines

God's answer: But his delight is in the law of the Lord; and in his law doth he meditate day and night. And he shall be like a tree planted by the rivers of water, that bringeth forth his fruit in his season; his leaf also shall not wither; and whatsoever he doeth shall prosper. (Psalms 1:2–3)

Comments and mini-report: The relationship of King's kids to the King is supposed to be the same as that of the natural branches (that's us) to the vine (that's Jesus).

That's the way Jesus describes it in John 15.

Have you ever tried to act as if you believed that was true?

Until I did, I was always in some sort of doubt as to just how I stood with God.

Was I being good enough?

Should I do more to please Him?

After every post-sermon invitation, I would routinely take myself to the altar and ask for prayer that I might serve Him better.

That was good—but I was missing the best. What was the best? *Victory* 131–35 tells you all about it.

Gravity, Winner 9–10
Grief, God's in Charge 16–17
Ground Energizer, Winner 49–53
Grounded Planes, Winner 49–53

Grumbling

God's answer: Do all things without murmurings and disputings: That ye may be blameless and harmless, the sons of God, without rebuke, in the midst of a crooked and perverse nation, among whom ye shine as lights in the world. (Philippians 2:14–15)

Fix your thoughts on what is true and good and right. Think about things that are pure and lovely, and dwell on the fine, good things in others. Think about all you can praise God for and be glad about. (Philippians 4:8 TLB)

For ye were sometimes darkness, but now are ye light in the Lord: walk as children of light. (Ephesians 5:8)

And when the people complained, it displeased the Lord. (Numbers 11:1a)

Comments and mini-report: Grumbling indicates a total disregard for God's promises and takes the soul—fast—into a state of heaviness. Who wants it?

God promises to give us victory in every circumstance of life if we will only change our attitude. But how, Lord? What is the antidote for grumbling?

If you don't know the answer to that one, read on—in *King's Kid* 207; *Victory* 69–70, 108.

Guidance (see also Eyeball Guidance)
God's answer: Let the word of Christ dwell in you richly in all wisdom. (Colossians 3:16a)

As newborn babes, desire the sincere milk of the word, that ye may grow thereby. (1 Peter 2:2)

Thy word is a lamp unto my feet, and a light unto my path. (Psalms 119:105)

These things that were written in the Scriptures so long ago are to teach us. (Romans 15:4 TLB)

Call unto me, and I will answer thee, and shew thee great and mighty things, which thou knowest not. (Jeremiah 33:3)

For this God is our God for ever and ever: he will be our guide even unto death. (Psalms 48:14)

Commit thy works unto the Lord, and thy thoughts shall be established. (Proverbs 16:3)

Comments and mini-report: Do you want a closer walk with Jesus?

Would you like to be in the center of His will at all times and really know it—for sure?

You can. As a matter of fact, that's God's plan for your life. How does it work?

Read on—in *Victory* 155–56, 263–68.

Guilt

God's answer: Brothers! Listen! In this man Jesus, there is forgiveness for your sins! Everyone who trusts in him is freed from all guilt and declared righteous. (Acts 13:38–39 TLB)

If we confess our sins, he is faithful and just to forgive us our sins, and to cleanse us from all unrighteousness. (1 John 1:9)

Come now, and let us reason together, saith the Lord: though your sins be as scarlet, they shall be as white as snow; though they be red like crimson, they shall be as wool. (Isaiah 1:18)

So overflowing is his kindness towards us that he took away all our sins through the blood of his Son, by whom we are saved. (Ephesians 1:7 TLB)

Comments and mini-report: Lots of King's kids leave planet earth prematurely because of cancer and other foul diseases.

How come?

They simply do not realize the connection between their body chemistry and the state of their souls.

The truth is that when the soul contains untreated guilt, or unhandled unforgiveness, the results filter into the body chemistry with destructive results.

Exactly how do these things work, and what can be done about them?

For openers, read *King's Kid* 18, 23–24, 201–2; *Goo* 75; *Winner* 63–69; *Victory* 198.

Guilt Trips, God's in Charge 13, 74–75, 100, 121–24
Gurick, Nick, Live the Bible 81–84

Hand-Me-Downs, God's in Charge 20, 22

Harvest

God's answer: Pray ye therefore the Lord of the harvest, that he will send forth labourers into his harvest. (Matthew 9:38)

And he saith unto them, Follow me, and I will make you fishers of men. (Matthew 4:19)

Not by might, nor by power, but by my spirit, saith the Lord of hosts. (Zechariah 4:6b)

Comments and mini-report: Have you ever wondered why God doesn't take us to heaven immediately after we get saved—before we have time to get into more messes?

I used to wonder about that. It seemed to me it would save a lot of misery if He would get us saved in front of a firing squad. Then, as soon as we'd received Jesus, He'd say, "Fire!" and in the twinkling of an eye we'd be home free. No more sin.

I don't think that way any more, though, because

I've learned that God has a plan for our lives right here. He begins to unfold that plan after we enter into a proper relationship with Him through His Son, Jesus. The plan has to do with fruit-bearing, which starts with seed-planting and ends up with a harvest of fruit.

"By their fruits ye shall know them" is always true in the test area of our lives.

For some of what I have learned about my part in all this, read *Victory* 143–48.

Head-on collisions. See **Highway Accidents**

Healing (see also **Communion; Laying On of Hands;** and names of specific ailments, for example, **Arthritis; Back Trouble; Cancer; Eyeball Ailments,** and so on) *God's answer:* Is any sick among you? let him call for the elders of the church; and let them pray over him, anointing him with oil in the name of the Lord: And the prayer of faith shall save the sick, and the Lord shall raise him up; and if he have committed sins, they shall be forgiven him. (James 5:14–15)

I pray that you will begin to understand how incredibly great his power is to help those who believe him. (Ephesians 1:19 TLB)

But he was wounded for our transgressions, he was bruised for our iniquities: the chastisement of our peace was upon him; and with his stripes we are healed. (Isaiah 53:5)

And heal the sick that are therein, and say unto them, The kingdom of God is come nigh unto you. (Luke 10:9)

For I will restore health unto thee, and I will heal thee of thy wounds, saith the Lord. (Jeremiah 30:17a)

Comments and mini-report: Medical science reports that many forms of cancer begin with broken person-to-person relationships.

Modern psychiatry teaches you how to repress guilt by denying that you are guilty. After all, the raunchy things you did were a part of human nature, weren't they?

God's antidote to guilt is forgiveness through the confession of sins. And He doesn't only forgive the sin—He goes on to cleanse us from all unrighteousness. You can't beat a deal like that.

For some case histories and more about healing, read *King's Kid* 99–112; *Victory* 105–17, 234; *God's in Charge* 71–80, 91–101, 121–25.

Hearing Loss, Live the Bible 124–25; God's in Charge 136

Heart Trouble
God's answer: Men's hearts failing them for fear, and for looking after those things which are coming on the earth. (Luke 21:26a)

Wherefore as the Holy Ghost saith, To day if ye will hear his voice, Harden not your hearts, as in the provocation, in the day of temptation in the wilderness. (Hebrews 3:7–8)

Come unto me, all ye that labour and are heavy laden, and I will give you rest. Take my yoke upon you, and learn of me; for I am meek and lowly in heart: and ye shall find rest unto your souls. For my yoke is easy, and my burden is light. (Matthew 11:28–30)

A new heart also will I give you, and a new spirit will I put within you: and I will take away the stony heart out of your flesh, and I will give you an heart of flesh. (Ezekiel 36:26)

Comments and mini-report: What will be your reaction when you are at the point of death from a heart ailment or any other terminal condition? I often wondered what my own reaction would be, even though I *knew* I knew I would be with Jesus almost instantaneously with my departure from planet earth.

And then one day it happened. Everything quit. No pulse, no blood pressure, no breathing. All systems halted, and I was on my way! Glory!

What happened next? Read all about it in *Winner* 189–93. There's also further interesting information about heart trouble in *Goo* 75–77.

Heavenly vitamins. See **Vitamins, Heavenly**
Heaven's Best, God's in Charge 128–40

Heroin

God's answer: For because he himself has suffered and been tempted, he is able to help those who are tempted. (Hebrews 2:18 RSV)

There hath no temptation taken you but such as is common to man: but God is faithful, who will not suffer you to be tempted above that ye are able; but will with the temptation also make a way to escape, that ye may be able to bear it. (1 Corinthians 10:13)

I will praise thee with my whole heart. . . . In the day when I cried thou answeredst me, and strengthenedst me with strength in my soul. (Psalms 138:1a, 3)

Comments and mini-report: When a federal law has been broken and the guilty person is before a relentless judge, is there any way out?

Can God override the opinion of a federal jurist when a verdict of "guilty as charged" would be completely in order?

Do King's kids really receive special attention from the Great Judge, God Himself?

They most certainly do, as King's kid Ralph James can report. Read about his case in *Winner* 39–47.

Hezekiah, King's Kid 68–69

Highway Accidents
God's answer: Fear thou not; for I am with thee: be not dismayed; for I am thy God: I will strengthen thee; yea, I will help thee; yea, I will uphold thee with the right hand of my righteousness. (Isaiah 41:10)

And the Lord, he it is that doth go before thee; he will be with thee, he will not fail thee, neither forsake thee: fear not, neither be dismayed. (Deuteronomy 31:8)

Then they cried unto the Lord in their trouble, and he delivered them out of their distresses. (Psalms 107:6)

Comments and mini-report: Can God intercede in the middle of certain death on the highway?

When a rear tire blows out and a car is completely out of control, can King's kids expect special care?

At the moment when a head-on collision is unavoidable, is there a way out?

God says there is, and He has proven it to me!

On both occasions, as death was but moments away, the mighty hand of the Almighty intervened.

How do I know for sure? I'm still here to prove it.

101

Read about these hair-raising adventures in *King's Kid* 112–16, 147–49. And check *God's in Charge* 60–63 for a case where an auto accident turned out to be better than no accident, all things considered.

Holy Spirit (see also **Baptism in the Holy Spirit; Gifts of the Holy Spirit**)
God's answer: But the Comforter, which is the Holy Ghost, whom the Father will send in my name, he shall teach you all things, and bring all things to your remembrance, whatsoever I have said unto you. (John 14:26)

Even the Spirit of truth; whom the world cannot receive, because it seeth him not, neither knoweth him: but ye know him: for he dwelleth with you, and shall be in you. (John 14:17)

But ye shall receive power, after that the Holy Ghost is come upon you: and ye shall be witnesses unto me both in Jerusalem and in all Judea, and in Samaria, and unto the uttermost part of the earth. (Acts 1:8)

Comments and mini-report: How is the Holy Spirit to be regarded in the life of a King's kid?
Is it true we receive all there is of the Holy Spirit at the moment of salvation, the moment when we invite Jesus to come in and take over? Or is there more to be had for the asking?
Are the gifts of the Holy Spirit still operating today? Are they for us? All of them?
Must all believers speak in new tongues?
Are tongues really from God?

You can know all these answers without a doubt from now on. Some of them are found in *King's Kid* 47; *Goo* 79–90; *Winner* 17–20. For answers to the rest of the questions, check this index under the headings **Baptism in the Holy Spirit; Gifts of the Holy Spirit; Tongues.**

Homosexuality

God's answer: Those who live immoral lives, who are idol worshipers, adulterers or homosexuals—will have no share in his kingdom. . . . There was a time when some of you were just like that but now your sins are washed away, and you are set apart for God, and he has accepted you because of what the Lord Jesus Christ and the Spirit of our God have done for you. (1 Corinthians 6:10–11 TLB)

Wherefore God also gave them up to uncleanness through the lusts of their own hearts, to dishonour their own bodies between themselves: Who changed the truth of God into a lie, and worshipped and served the creature more than the Creator, who is blessed for ever. Amen. For this cause God gave them up unto vile affections: for even their women did change the natural use into that which is against nature: And likewise also the men, leaving the natural use of the woman, burned in their lust one toward another; men with men working that which is unseemly, and receiving in themselves that recompence of their error which was meet. (Romans 1:24–27)

Comments and mini-report: Exactly what is homosexuality? Is it just a bad habit? Or is it a sin?

Lots of controversy rages about this expanding situation.

Could it be there's a demon in charge?

103

The man in this situation was not so much concerned with causes. He wanted deliverance. And he
got it.

When the demon came out of him. . . .

Read all about it in *Winner* 59–60.

Horoscopes

God's answer: Don't act like the people who make
horoscopes and try to read their fate and future in
the stars! Don't be frightened by predictions such as
theirs, for it is all a pack of lies. Their ways are futile
and foolish. (Jeremiah 10:2–3 TLB)

Comments and mini-report: "I don't see anything
wrong with reading the daily horoscope" is a remark I
hear frequently these days.

Generally, the persons have come for answers to
their emotionally distressed state. When I learn that
they've been consulting the astrology columns and
explain that's an underlying reason for their below-
the-wormholes outlook on life, they are dumbfounded.

"But I don't take it *seriously,*" they sputter, trying to
laugh it off. But the chuckles don't sound sincere—
even to them—and some of them take my word for it
that letting the stars tell you what to do tomorrow—
even in fun—opens your soul for a full-scale invasion
of the boys in black. Satan comes to kill and to destroy, we know. No wonder horoscope readers can
readily develop suicidal tendencies! The result is built
into the system.

If you're still not persuaded to close your eyes to the
horoscope page in your daily scandal sheet, read these
further warnings in *King's Kid* 182; *Winner* 149, 183,
187–88; *Victory* 296.

Hot line to heaven. See **Tongues**

Hotel No-Vacancy Signs, Winner 113–20; Victory 227–30; Live the Bible 113–17

Hunger, Flab 75–85

Hurricanes, Victory 219–21

Husband-Wife Haggles (see also **Divorce; Fractured Marriage**)

God's answer: Wives, submit yourselves unto your own husbands, as unto the Lord. For the husband is the head of the wife, even as Christ is the head of the church: and he is the saviour of the body. Therefore as the church is subject unto Christ, so let the wives be to their own husbands in every thing. (Ephesians 5:22–24)

Husbands, love your wives, even as Christ also loved the church, and gave himself for it; That he might sanctify and cleanse it with the washing of water by the word, That he might present it to himself a glorious church, not having spot, or wrinkle, or any such thing: but that it should be holy and without blemish. So ought men to love their wives as their own bodies. He that loveth his wife loveth himself. (Ephesians 5:25–28)

Comments and mini-report: "Submit to me or else!" is the sick attitude in many homes today.

"Submit to one another in love" is God's antidote for most family rhubarbs.

Have you ever consciously set out to respect your mate's right to be wrong?

I tried this technique on my wife, and it worked wonders.

And what's even more amazing, she actually began to be right once in a while!

For more about husband-wife haggles, read *Victory* 173–85, 193–94; *God's in Charge* 22–24, 40–48.

Icky Prayer List, Winner 185; Victory 89
Iffy doctrines. See **False Teaching**

Ignorance

God's answer: For they being ignorant of God's righteousness, and going about to establish their own righteousness, have not submitted themselves unto the righteousness of God. (Romans 10:3)

Having the understanding darkened, being alienated from the life of God through the ignorance that is in them, because of the blindness of their heart. (Ephesians 4:18)

But the natural man receiveth not the things of the Spirit of God: for they are foolishness unto him: neither can he know them, because they are spiritually discerned. But he that is spiritual judgeth all things, yet he himself is judged of no man. (1 Corinthians 2:14–15)

Now concerning spiritual gifts, brethren, I would not have you ignorant. (1 Corinthians 12:1)

Comments and mini-report: Ignorance is not the same thing as innocence. Ignorance is willfully ignoring truth and acting in the opposite direction.

Now, innocence is excused by God, and often the "many deserved stripes" wind up being just a "few."

But willful ignorance, which is rebellion, is "as the sin of witchcraft"! And it can be punished accordingly.

Ignorance of spiritual gifts—ignoring them in your

own life—might constitute a problem if continued too long!

To avoid pitfalls, read up on ignorance in *King's Kid* 173; *Victory* 84, 269–75.

Impatience (see also **Fullness of Time**)

God's answer: Don't be impatient for the Lord to act! Keep traveling steadily along his pathway and in due season he will honor you with every blessing. (Psalms 37:34 TLB)

Wherefore seeing we also are compassed about with so great a cloud of witnesses, let us lay aside every weight, and the sin which doth so easily beset us, and let us run with patience the race that is set before us, Looking unto Jesus the author and finisher of our faith. (Hebrews 12:1–2a)

Strengthened with all might, according to his glorious power, unto all patience and longsuffering with joyfulness. (Colossians 1:11)

But the fruit of the Spirit is love, joy, peace, patience, kindness, goodness, faithfulness, gentleness and self-control. (Galatians 5:22 RSV)

Comments and mini-report: Have you ever had trouble simply waiting on God?

Does it seem sometimes that God is hard of hearing?

Or that He doesn't pay any attention to your prayers?

Have you ever prayed, asked God to bless what you were about to do, run out and done it, and then fallen flat on your face—and blamed God for the disaster?

Sure you have. So did I, until I learned something about His ways.

Impatience leads to discouragement, and a discouraged King's kid is a mess. Read up on these things and avoid the traps. Try *Winner* 16, 153; *Victory* 57–58, 127, 154–55, 205–11.

Incubation. See **Brooding**
Iniquity. See **Guilt**

Insanity

God's answer: These things I have spoken unto you, that in me ye might have peace. In the world ye shall have tribulation: but be of good cheer; I have overcome the world. (John 16:33)

For whatsoever is born of God overcometh the world: and this is the victory that overcometh the world, even our faith. Who is he that overcometh the world, but he that believeth that Jesus is the Son of God? (1 John 5:4–5)

I will not leave you comfortless: I will come to you. (John 14:18)

Comments and mini-report: What is insanity? Is it a mental illness? Or does it have something to do with demonic power?

Modern religion says demons are simply a figure of speech. Psychiatry giggles at the very idea.

But when your wife is locked up in a "head hospital" with no hope for recovery—ever—you don't quibble. You look for what works to get her out of there and into her right mind.

Gloria (not her name) was in that state. Her husband didn't care what caused it—he just wanted his wife back.

When the two demons came out of her, it would

have been hard to say they were only a "figure of speech." At least, you'd have a hard time convincing Gloria's husband the demons weren't real, because when they left, he got his wife back! Read all about it in *King's Kid* 189–95. And if you want to know how *my* wife got into the kooky bin—and out again—read *King's Kid* 181–83. For the pastureland diet that cured Nebuchadnezzar of *his* craziness, try *Flab* 63.

Insomnia

God's answer: . . . He giveth his beloved sleep. (Psalms 127:2)

Comments and mini-report: When Jack couldn't sleep, we prayed. Jack's snoozing improved radically, of course, and in the midst of it, God opened my eyes. Read all about it in *Live the Bible* 11–13.

Intensive Care

God's answer: Casting all your care upon him; for he careth for you. (1 Peter 5:7)

We know that all things work together for good to them that love God, to them who are the called according to his purpose. (Romans 8:28)

Comments and mini-report: "What a shame a King's kid had to spend time in a cardiac intensive care unit!" someone said sympathetically after I came out of the hospital.

It's a plain fact that King's kids are limited in their intensive-care-unit ministries unless they are horizontal, twenty-four-hour-a-day inhabitants of those places.

The good Lord permitted me two trips to ICU of one week each—a new King's kid adventure.

The reason? That showed up after I got there. God seldom gives ahead-of-time reasons for His manipulation of our experiences. He simply says, "Trust Me," and then every experience becomes an adventure for His glory and our blessing.

So, the man in the next bed heard about Jesus, and I expect to see him up yonder. One more proof that nothing accidental ever happens to this King's kid! For the ICU story, read *Winner* 191–93.

Intercessory prayer. See **Prayer, Intercessory**

Interpretation of Tongues

God's answer: Wherefore let him that speaketh in an unknown tongue pray that he may interpret. What is it then? I will pray with the spirit, and I will pray with the understanding also: I will sing with the spirit, and I will sing with the understanding also. (1 Corinthians 14:13, 15)

Comments and mini-report: Is interpretation of tongues a literal translation of the message? Nope, hardly ever.

Is tongues really all that important in the life of a King's kid? How else are you going to pray without ceasing?

Can this gift sometimes be from the wrong source? Must we be very careful that deception not creep in?

These are all good questions; you need the answers. "Ask, seek, knock, and test the spirits" is the advice of Jesus concerning these matters.

Actually, interpretation of tongues is generally a response from God to the message just received from the Holy Spirit. That's why the message and the interpretation may be of widely varying lengths and of totally different structure.

Why does God do it this crazy way? *None of your business!* It's all *His* business, and when we receive His gifts in meekness and humility, not putting ourselves above God, we're in a position to receive real blessing on the way to glory!

Read more about interpretation of tongues in *King's Kid* 136, 158, 194; *Victory* 235.

Inventions. See Ground Energizer

Jailbirds, Live the Bible 123–24

Jehovah's Witnesses

God's answer: But there were false prophets also among the people, even as there shall be false teachers among you, who privily shall bring in damnable heresies, even denying the Lord that bought them, and bring upon themselves swift destruction. And many shall follow their pernicious ways; by reason of whom the way of truth shall be evil spoken of. (2 Peter 2:1–2)

Comments and mini-report: How do you combat error when you come eyeball-to-eyeball with it?

Should a King's kid memorize all the errors of all the cults in order to effectively combat them?

How much do we need to know in order to prove that Jehovah's Witnesses are in error?

God's answer is not complicated. Jesus simply says, "Lift Me up, and I'll draw all men to Myself."

The man at the door was there to persuade me to join his cult. As a new Christian, I knew very little about it except that it held no hope of salvation for me. "The quota is only 144,000," they say, "and it's already filled—with a long waiting list."

How can you lead a JW man to Jesus? I wondered.

I already knew that human reason never changes religious thinking. Argument loses every time.

But God had a plan—and Jesus never fails! Read about it in *King's Kid* 59–63.

Jeremiah, Victory 53–54
Jesze, George, Live the Bible 90–104
Jewish Spiritists, Winner 71–77
Job, Victory 112, 160–61; God's in Charge 74, 149
Job loss. See **Unemployment**
Joni, God's in Charge 99
Joshua, King's Kid 66–67; Goo 72–73; Victory 32

Judging

God's answer: Therefore thou art inexcusable, O man, whosoever thou art that judgest: for wherein thou judgest another, thou condemnest thyself; for thou that judgest doest the same things. (Romans 2:1)

And why beholdest thou the mote that is in thy brother's eye, but considerest not the beam that is in thine own eye? (Matthew 7:3)

Comments and mini-report: Judgment comes on two levels—the natural and the spiritual.

Natural judging of others simply acknowledges our own problems, according to the mirror principle of God's Word.

Judging in terms of Scripture is God's safeguard for King's kids in action so they won't fall into deception.

Learning to judge "righteous judgment" is a necessary instrument in the working tools of King's kids in action.

Become proficient in this area and avoid the traps of the enemy.

For further instructions, read *Victory* 65–67, 258–59; *God's in Charge* 56–59.

Knowledge. See **Word of Knowledge**

Labyrinthitis, Live the Bible 124
Lack of power. See **Power Shortage**

Landing-Gear Malfunction
God's answer: Rejoice evermore. Pray without ceasing. In every thing give thanks: for this is the will of God in Christ Jesus concerning you. (1 Thessalonians 5:16–18)

Have not I commanded thee? Be strong and of a good courage; be not afraid, neither be thou dismayed: for the Lord thy God is with thee whithersoever thou goest. (Joshua 1:9)

Comments and mini-report: "Brace yourselves for a belly landing," came the instructions from the pilot as our plane prepared to land without wheels that wintry night at Kennedy Airport in New York.

"Hey! A jet prop usually catches on fire from the friction heat during a belly landing!" I reminded myself. "That means this could be graduation day!"

That realization *could* have made me nervous, but I knew where I was going when my earth time was up, so I was excited instead.

"Make it quick and easy, please, Jesus," was my only request.

Then came His directive. "Not so fast, Hill. Some folks on this flight aren't saved yet. Intercede, for *their* sakes."

I prayed, He heard, He answered. Can God fix inoperable landing gears? He sure can. Don't believe it? Read the report in *King's Kid* 1–6.

Language Barrier

God's answer: But whatsoever shall be given you in that hour, that speak ye: for it is not ye that speak, but the Holy Ghost. (Mark 13:11b)

For the Holy Ghost shall teach you in the same hour what ye ought to say. (Luke 12:12)

Trust in the Lord with all thine heart; and lean not unto thine own understanding. In all thy ways acknowledge him, and he shall direct thy paths. (Proverbs 3:5–6)

Open thy mouth wide, and I will fill it. (Psalms 81:10b)

Comments and mini-report: As a new Christian, I heard that the gift of tongues was not for today. Some people even said that the strange-sounding words came from evil spirits.

Others said tongues might be for some folks today but that they served no useful purpose and generally caused a heap of trouble.

But when language barriers need to be broken and there is no way to communicate in a foreign land, it is mighty useful when the Holy Spirit gives words that solve the problem.

I was lost in Germany with no way to communicate. "Lord," I prayed, "please give me a word in German—any word."

He did better than that—He gave me two words. And saved the day for me.

This kind of thing has happened on numerous occasions to this King's kid—and others. For my two words, read the account in *Winner* 130–32. For other accounts of God-to-the-rescue communication, try *King's Kid* 85–87; *Winner* 1–8; *Live the Bible* 109–12.

Laser Beam

God's answer: For the word of God is quick, and powerful, and sharper than any two edged sword, piercing even to the dividing asunder of soul and spirit, and of the joints and marrow, and is a discerner of the thoughts and intents of the heart. (Hebrews 4:12)

Comments and mini-report: A laser beam is highly concentrated energy which is used for bloodless surgery, among other things. Extremely delicate operations, such as sewing back into place detached retinas of the eye, are possible with lasers.

Lasers can also be used to destroy life by simply destroying living cells with their high intensity energy. Through an accidental overexposure to such high intensity light energy, the eyesight in my left eye was destroyed as my retina was burned by reflected laser energy.

God is light, and His intensely concentrated energy (power) is used by the Holy Spirit to perform bloodless surgery on our souls and bring wholeness in spirit, soul, and body.

How does it work? Read all about it in *Victory* 37–39.

Lawsuits

God's answer: If we confess our sins, he is faithful and just to forgive us our sins, and to cleanse us from all unrighteousness. (1 John 1:9)

Offer unto God thanksgiving; and pay thy vows unto the most High: And call upon me in the day of trouble: I will deliver thee, and thou shalt glorify me. (Psalms 50:14–15)

Comments and mini-report: Should King's kids take people to court to settle disputes? Isn't it a good thing to stand up for your own rights?

Or is there a better way to get your money back when someone refuses to pay a past debt?

God says a lot about these things in His Word, and I have experienced some of them and thereby learned the "better way."

My friend Rodney had owed me a large sum for many years. When I asked for payment of the loan, he flew into a rage and screamed, "Sue me! Sue me!"

"I'll do just that very thing!" I retorted, banging the door as I went out.

But then the Holy Spirit began to speak to my heart and I became a winner—God's way.

Read all about it in *Winner* 80–82. For another case where God averted a certain lawsuit, read *King's Kid* 133–37.

Laying On of Hands

God's answer: These signs shall follow them that believe; In my name . . . they shall lay hands on the sick, and they shall recover. (Mark 16:17–18)

Comments and mini-report: The Word of God has a lot to say about the laying on of hands for healing. It isn't always necessary to lay hands on the sick for them to recover, but sometimes it helps.

When Oral Roberts laid hands on me in June of 1954 when I needed healing of a serious spinal ailment, he explained to me in simple terms how these things work.

"I have no power to heal or even to help you in any way," he said. "It is God who does the healing, not me. But if my hands can be a point of contact for releasing your faith, I'll be glad to lay them on you."

116

It was all new to me, but it made sense. Even if it hadn't made sense, I'd have been willing to try it because my back felt so bad and God's Word in Mark 16:17–18 sounded so good.

What happened? A miracle! Read all about it in *King's Kid* 39–40. More about the laying on of hands in *King's Kid* 99–105, 175–77; *Winner* 30, 101–6; *Victory* 97–98, 102–3, 237.

Lazarus, God's in Charge 31–32, 113
Leukemia, Winner 64–69
Liebman's Glory Meter, Goo 81–86

Light

God's answer: Then spake Jesus again unto them, saying, I am the light of the world: he that followeth me shall not walk in darkness, but shall have the light of life. (John 8:12)

But if we walk in the light, as he is in the light, we have fellowship one with another, and the blood of Jesus Christ his Son cleanseth us from all sin. (1 John 1:7)

For ye were sometimes darkness, but now are ye light in the Lord: walk as children of light. (Ephesians 5:8)

And the city had no need of the sun, neither of the moon, to shine in it: for the glory of God did lighten it, and the Lamb is the light thereof. (Revelation 21:23)

Comments and mini-report: When God said, "Let there be light," He created not just that band of visible light contained in the one octave we can see with our eyes. At the same time, He brought into being the whole spectrum of wavelengths of which the entire universe—and everything in it, including you—is made up.

Blows your mind? It should! Ours is a wonder-working God! And walking in the light of God's presence in the *now* insures protection from all the powers of darkness—forever!

Read more about God's light in *King's Kid* 116; *Goo* 22–23, 82, 86–89; *Winner* 180; *Victory* 95, 300.

Lions

God's answer: My God hath sent his angel, and hath shut the lions' mouths, that they have not hurt me.... (Daniel 6:22)

Comments and mini-report: You already know that God shut the lions' mouths for Daniel, but did you know that He did the same thing for a friend of mine? Read all about this hair-raising adventure in *God's in Charge* 102–4. More about lions in *Victory* 189–91.

Lost in Strange Surroundings

God's answer: Yes, be bold and strong! Banish fear and doubt! For remember, the Lord your God is with you wherever you go. (Joshua 1:9 TLB)

If any of you lack wisdom, let him ask of God ... and it shall be given him. (James 1:5)

And thine ears shall hear a word behind thee, saying, This is the way, walk ye in it, when ye turn to the right hand, and when ye turn to the left. (Isaiah 30:21)

Comments and mini-report: When the directions you have been given are wrong, when road maps are no help, and there is no way to turn, does God come to the rescue of King's kids?

He certainly does, and in the most unusual ways!

The man who was to guide me to a meeting was taken ill, and I found myself stranded in the center of New York City without a single clue as to my next move.

Suddenly, from seemingly nowhere, there appeared a little man dressed in obviously foreign clothing. In heavily accented English he asked, "Someone want go Long Island?"

That was the general direction I needed to go—but just how did the odd little man fit into God's plans for me?

Read all about it in *Victory* 309–12. For a further account of how God got me unlost in strange surroundings, read *Winner* 127–33; *Live the Bible* 59–62.

Lost Key, Live the Bible 93–104

Love

God's answer: Now you can have real love for everyone because your souls have been cleansed from selfishness and hatred when you trusted Christ to save you; so see to it that you really do love each other warmly, with all your hearts. (1 Peter 1:22 TLB)

The love of God is shed abroad in our hearts by the Holy Ghost which is given unto us. (Romans 5:5b)

And the Lord make you to increase and abound in love one toward another, and toward all men, even as we do toward you. (1 Thessalonians 3:12)

But when the Holy Spirit controls our lives he will produce this kind of fruit in us: love. . . . (Galatians 5:22 TLB)

119

He that loveth not knoweth not God; for God is love. (1 John 4:8)

And to know the love of Christ, which passeth knowledge, that ye might be filled with all the fulness of God. (Ephesians 3:19)

Comments and mini-report: Does God love us for our goodness, obedience, sinlessness, or our diligence in Bible study?

Of course not. He loves us because He *is* love.

Trying to "stay saved" through trying to deserve God's love misses the blessing every time.

Trusting God for who He is—sovereign God—is the gateway to glory!

Read more about His love in *King's Kid* 56; *Victory* 84–87, 181–82.

LSD

God's answer: All things are lawful unto me, but all things are not expedient: all things are lawful for me, but I will not be brought under the power of any. (1 Corinthians 6:12)

Be sober, be vigilant; because your adversary the devil, as a roaring lion, walketh about, seeking whom he may devour. (1 Peter 5:8)

Now thanks be unto God, which always causeth us to triumph in Christ, and maketh manifest the savour of his knowledge by us in every place. (2 Corinthians 2:14)

Greater is he that is in you, than he that is in the world. (1 John 4:4b)

Comments and mini-report: As we prayed for a young man afflicted with total loss of motivation to live, the Holy Spirit—through the gift of discerning of spirits—revealed the cause of his trouble: tripping on LSD!

In fact, God even revealed the true manifestation of this drug as He sees it—leprosy of the soul. He let me see it, too! Down inside the boy, I "saw" in the spirit this foul, ghastly white monster eating away at his soul and robbing him of all interest in life.

We then applied the spiritual tools which God has provided for combating these things. Result? Read about it in *Winner* 143–47.

Lust

God's answer: For all that is in the world, the lust of the flesh, and the lust of the eyes, and the pride of life, is not of the Father, but is of the world. (1 John 2:16)

Comments and mini-report: Lust is not necessarily concerned with something that is sinful in itself. It is simply the attitude, "I must have this for my own satisfaction right now, regardless of the effect of my actions on others."

Lust demands instant gratification in two areas—eyes and flesh—and is a soulish drive for completeness in things. Lust may carry over into the spiritual life without ever appearing on the surface at all.

Desire to fill the teaching job in Sunday school may come from either lust for recognition or from a sincere desire to serve God and the brethren.

How can lust be detected? Only by the Word of God which is the only instrument sharp enough to separate the thoughts from the intents of the heart.

Read more about lust in *Victory* 77.

Machinery repair. See **Technical Difficulties**

Manifest Sons of God

God's answer: Beloved, believe not every spirit, but try the spirits whether they are of God: because many false prophets are gone out into the world. Hereby know ye the Spirit of God: Every spirit that confesseth that Jesus Christ is come in the flesh is of God: And every spirit that confesseth not that Jesus Christ is come in the flesh is not of God: and this is that spirit of antichrist, whereof ye have heard that it should come; and even now already is it in the world. Ye are of God, little children, and have overcome them: because greater is he that is in you, than he that is in the world. They are of the world: therefore speak they of the world, and the world heareth them. We are of God: he that knoweth God heareth us; he that is not of God heareth not us. Hereby know we the spirit of truth, and the spirit of error. (1 John 4:1–6)

Comments and mini-report: Of the many satanic cults active in these latter times, the one called Manifest Sons of God is probably the most devastating. Appealing to the human ego, it makes man out to be sinlessly perfect, incapable of committing sin.

When emissaries of this movement came to our church several years ago, they enticed a number of our members into their devilish doctrine of sinless perfection.

Many families were destroyed, families broken, and marriages wrecked.

Awareness of such things helps us avoid their pitfalls. Further details in *Victory* 284–90.

Manufacturer's Handbook

God's answer: All scripture is given by inspiration of

God, and is profitable for doctrine, for reproof, for correction, for instruction in righteousness. (2 Timothy 3:16)

Knowing this first, that no prophecy of the scripture is of any private interpretation. For the prophecy came not in old time by the will of man: but holy men of God spake as they were moved by the Holy Ghost. (2 Peter 1:20–21)

Heaven and earth shall pass away, but my words shall not pass away. (Matthew 24:35)

Thy word is truth. (John 17:17b)

Comments and mini-report: What should be our attitude toward the Bible?

I asked this question of many church members when I became a Christian about thirty years ago. Some said, "Take it literally, word for word." At the other extreme there were those who warned me about being too serious about a book which had passed through so many hands over the centuries. "It could be full of error," they warned.

My attitude? I decided to try this one: "The Bible is the *Manufacturer's Handbook,* written expressly for me by my very own heavenly Father." In other words, the Bible became, for me, the Manufacturer Himself speaking to His product—a King's kid.

What an adventure my life has been since then! Reading the Bible and doing it makes for the most exciting life imaginable!

What should the *Manufacturer's Handbook* be for you? Read all about it in *King's Kid* 25–26, 31; *Goo* 17; *Winner* 10, 15–16; *Victory* 83, 122–23, 136–39; *Live the Bible* 24–26.

Mediums

God's answer: There shall not be found among you anyone who makes his son or his daughter pass through the fire, one who uses divination, one who practices witchcraft, or one who interprets omens, or a sorcerer, or one who casts a spell, or a medium, or a spiritist, or one who calls up the dead. For whoever does these things is detestable to the Lord. (Deuteronomy 18:10–12a NAS)

I will set my face against anyone who consults mediums and wizards instead of me and I will cut that person off from his people. (Leviticus 20:6 TLB)

Comments and mini-report: "What's wrong with the occult anyway?" is a question I frequently hear from King's kids.

"But why not communicate with the spirit of dead Aunt Tillie? What's wrong with that?" some want to know.

"I don't see a thing wrong with reading the daily horoscope. After all, I don't *really* take it seriously," others reason.

You won't see anything wrong, and you won't take it seriously—until it's too late. Then you'll realize that *it* has taken *you* by inviting Satan to take over control of your reasoning powers and land you in an insane asylum.

Think I'm leaping to conclusions? Listen! My wife dabbled in such things and it cost us a year in institutions and untold torment. Be warned! Read *King's Kid* 180–82; *Winner* 71–77.

Mennonites, King's Kid 84–85
Mercedes-Benz, King's Kid 125–33; Live the Bible 37–43
Mexican Bean Pickers, Winner 1–8

Miracles

God's answer: For to one is given by the Spirit the word of wisdom . . . To another the working of miracles. (1 Corinthians 12:8a, 10a)

But as many as received him, to them gave he power to become the sons of God, even to them that believe on his name. (John 1:12)

Verily, verily, I say unto you, He that believeth on me, the works that I do shall he do also: and greater works than these shall he do; because I go unto my Father. (John 14:12)

Now you have every grace and blessing; every spiritual gift and power for doing his will are yours during this time of waiting for the return of our Lord Jesus Christ. (1 Corinthians 1:7 TLB)

Jesus said unto him, If thou canst believe, all things are possible to him that believeth. (Mark 9:23)

Comments and mini-report: When God decides to answer prayers in ways outside the normal course of things, we call them miracles.

Are miracles still happening today? One of the gifts

of the Holy Spirit has to do with just such things.

You haven't seen any miracles? Why not, I wonder? Have a look at a few recorded in the pages of *King's Kid* 152–55, 189–95; *Victory* 235, 273, 307; *Live the Bible* 120–21.

Mirror Principle, Victory 65–67; God's in Charge 44

Missing Day

God's answer: And the sun stood still, and the moon stayed, until the people had avenged themselves upon their enemies. Is not this written in the book of Jasher? So the sun stood still in the midst of heaven, and hasted not to go down about a whole day. (Joshua 10:13)

And Isaiah the prophet cried unto the Lord: and he brought the shadow ten degrees backward, by which it had gone down in the dial of Ahaz. (2 Kings 20:11)

Comments and mini-report: Can a computer actually locate a day missing for centuries and accounted for nowhere but in the Bible?

Did space scientists really acknowledge the Bible to be of value in their search for those elusive twenty-four hours?

Controversy over this question has raged ever since I reported on what happened at NASA headquarters at the Goddard Space Flight Center at Greenbelt, Maryland, several years ago.

Now you can read the whole story in *King's Kid* 65–77.

Missing key. See **Castle, Locked-Up**
Missing Sword, Live the Bible 65–67, 86

Negative Confession (see also **Brooding; Reacting vs. Responding; Unbelief**)

God's answer: Death and life are in the power of the tongue. (Proverbs 18:21a)

A wholesome tongue is a tree of life: but perverseness therein is a breach in the spirit. (Proverbs 15:4)

Set a watch, O Lord, before my mouth; keep the door of my lips. (Psalms 141:3)

Comments and mini-report: "You have what you say," is not all myth.

Do you witness to the negatives in life, always grumbling and complaining? Is your testimony locked in on your troubles?

If so, they will increase. Guaranteed.

But wrapping everything in praise and turning it over to Jesus brings amazing results.

Read more about how it works in *Victory* 69, 222–24.

For the unbelievably bad results of negative confession, read *Live the Bible* 97–100.

Nervous Imbalance, King's Kid 173–77
New creation. See **Born Again, How to Be**

New Management

God's answer: Therefore if any man be in Christ, he is a new creature: old things are passed away; behold, all things are become new. And all things are of God, who hath reconciled us to himself by Jesus Christ, and hath given to us the ministry of reconciliation. (2 Corinthians 5:17–18)

But we have this treasure in earthen vessels, that the excellency of the power may be of God, and not of us. (2 Corinthians 4:7)

I am crucified with Christ: nevertheless I live; yet not I, but Christ liveth in me: and the life which I now live in the flesh I live by the faith of the Son of God, who loved me, and gave himself for me. (Galatians 2:20)

Comments and mini-report: After twenty-nine years of doing my "own thing" and experiencing many top-level successes, I became sick and tired of being sick and tired and turned my life over to Jesus.

Life under the New Management has been progressively more of an adventure ever since. With the New Manager, Jesus, in charge, it's a relief to go to Him with my mistakes.

"Lord, I've goofed again. Continue to change me, or I'll goof some more."

So far, He hasn't given up on me, and I've watched

Him change the motives of my heart and bring them into closer conformity to His perfect will in my life.

Can it happen to you? Here's how: *King's Kid* 14; *Goo* 89–90; *Winner* xv, 13; *Victory* 218; *Live the Bible* 31–35; *God's in Charge* 38–39.

Nit-picking. See Grumbling; Husband-Wife Haggles
Noah, Goo 56–59
No-Nos for Flab Flippers, Flab 59–74
Nutrition, Flab 59–74

Obedience (see also **Doing God's Will**)
God's answer: And Samuel said, Hath the Lord as great delight in burnt offerings and sacrifices, as in obeying the voice of the Lord? Behold, to obey is better than sacrifice, and to hearken than the fat of rams. (1 Samuel 15:22)

Blessed rather are those who hear the word of God and obey it. (Luke 11:28 NIV)

God blesses those who obey him; happy the man who puts his trust in the Lord. (Proverbs 16:20 TLB)

And when we obey him, every path he guides us on is fragrant with his lovingkindness and his truth. (Psalms 25:10 TLB)

But if you stay in me and obey my commands, you may ask any request you like, and it will be granted! (John 15:7 TLB)

Comments and mini-report: God's emphasis on obedience is not to take away our fun but to shift our "druthers" so we'd druther do His will than our own.

How does that work?

You'll never know until you try it. Willingness to do God's will opens the door of the heart for His Spirit to work in us that which we can never know before we submit to Jesus.

Afterward, we'll hear ourselves saying, "Why did I wait so long?"

Read more about obedience in *Victory* 70–71, 153–55, 162–65; *Flab* 38–43.

Obstetrics, Heavenly, Victory 133, 260
Occult. See **Automatic Writing; Horoscopes; Mediums; Ouija Boards; Witchcraft**
Old Folks' Homes, Victory 227–30

Ouija Boards

God's answer: There shall not be found among you anyone who makes his son or his daughter pass through the fire, one who uses divination, one who practices witchcraft, or one who interprets omens, or a sorcerer, or one who casts a spell, or a medium, or a spiritist, or one who calls up the dead. For whoever does these things is detestable to the Lord. (Deuteronomy 18:10–12a NAS)

Comments and mini-report: Bait is always made to look attractive, and the bait employed by the enemy of our souls is no exception.

"What can possibly be wrong with a little old Ouija board?" many Christians ask, in total ignorance of the tricks of the enemy.

In addition to going against God's will when we attempt to delve into the future, or to communicate with the spirit world, we have found that any accessories— Ouija boards, crystal balls, tea leaves—expressly designed for such activities carry the spirit of the originator of that program.

130

Sounds farfetched, doesn't it? That's what a family in our church fellowship thought until the demons inhabiting their Ouija board went screaming up the chimney when the family burned it in the fireplace.

More warnings about Ouija boards in *King's Kid* 179; *Winner* 149, 183–84; *Victory* 296.

Overcomers, Winner xii–xiii
Overdose, King's Kid 152–55

Overeating
God's answer: Bless the Lord, O my soul, and forget not all his benefits: Who satisfieth thy mouth with good things; so that thy youth is renewed like the eagle's. (Psalms 103:2, 5)

And seek not ye what ye shall eat, or what ye shall drink, neither be ye of doubtful mind. (Luke 12:29)

Therefore I say unto you, Take no thought for your life, what ye shall eat, or what ye shall drink; nor yet for your body, what ye shall put on. Is not the life more than meat, and the body than raiment? (Matthew 6:25)

Comments and mini-report: Just having lost thirty-six pounds of excess flab, I'm in a position to speak with authority to this problem which afflicts so many King's kids.

Having tired of applying many fasts and diets, knowing somehow that the flab would return—as it always had before—I gave up and turned the whole mess over to Jesus.

The result? I began to drop one pound a week and have now arrived at my ideal weight—with no threat of return.

131

How? Read my book *How to Flip Your Flab—Forever*. In the meantime, send a self-addressed, stamped envelope for the secret formula the Lord gave me for weight reduction. Address: King's Kids' Korner, P.O. Box 8655, Baltimore, MD 21240.

More about overeating in *Victory* 77; *God's in Charge* 64.

Overweight. See **Flabbitis**

Ownership vs. Stewardship

God's answer: The earth is the Lord's, and the fulness thereof; the world, and they that dwell therein. (Psalms 24:1)

For of him, and through him, and to him, are all things: to whom be glory for ever. Amen. (Romans 11:36)

For what is a man profited, if he shall gain the whole world, and lose his own soul? (Matthew 16:26a)

Lay not up for yourselves treasures upon earth, where moth and rust doth corrupt, and where thieves break through and steal: But lay up for yourselves treasures in heaven, where neither moth nor rust doth corrupt, and where thieves do not break through nor steal: For where your treasure is, there will your heart be also. (Matthew 6:19–21)

And he said unto them, Take heed, and beware of covetousness: for a man's life consisteth not in the abundance of the things which he possesseth. (Luke 12:15)

Comments and mini-report: Owners have real problems protecting their rights, increasing their holdings,

132

and maintaining their position against those who would steal.

Stewards have no such problems. When danger threatens, they can go to their bosses and say, "Sir, *you* have a problem. What are *you* going to do about it, sir?"

How simple and stress-free life becomes with Jesus in charge!

More on this subject in *King's Kid* 149–55; *Winner* xvii–xix, 82–83, 165–66, 169–74; *Victory* 72–74, 78–81.

Pacifist, King's Kid 167–71
Pain, Winner 29–32; Live the Bible 69–84

Paralysis of Analysis
God's answer: For if any be a hearer of the word, and not a doer, he is like unto a man beholding his natural face in a glass: For he beholdeth himself, and goeth his way, and straightway forgetteth what manner of man he was. But whoso looketh into the perfect law of liberty, and continueth therein, he being not a forgetful hearer, but a doer of the work, this man shall be blessed in his deed. (James 1:23–25)

But the natural man receiveth not the things of the Spirit of God: for they are foolishness unto him: neither can he know them, because they are spiritually discerned. (1 Corinthians 2:14)

Beware lest any man spoil you through philosophy and vain deceit, after the tradition of men, after the rudiments of the world, and not after Christ. (Colossians 2:8)

Comments and mini-report: Why do most King's kids settle for second best instead of holding out for God's best?

Very simply—they refuse to do the Bible thing.

Just what is the Bible thing? To read the Word of God and do it—without questioning.

Analyzing the Word prior to doing anything about it leads to a do-nothing condition. Be doers of the Word to get the best from life here and hereafter.

Check it out in *King's Kid* xi.

Parkinson's Disease, God's in Charge 97–98
Patience. See **Impatience**
Paul, the Apostle, Victory 306–7; Live the Bible 89–90; God's in Charge 113, 140–43
Paula, Sister, Live the Bible 83–86

Peace
God's answer: Thou wilt keep him in perfect peace, whose mind is stayed on thee: because he trusteth in thee. (Isaiah 26:3)

Peace I leave with you, my peace I give unto you: not as the world giveth, give I unto you. Let not your heart be troubled, neither let it be afraid. (John 14:27)

And the very God of peace sanctify you wholly; and I pray God your whole spirit and soul and body be preserved blameless unto the coming of our Lord Jesus Christ. (1 Thessalonians 5:23)

Comments and mini-report: According to God's Word, peace is a portion of the fruit of the Spirit. Peace down inside is also a condition of wholeness promised by Jesus to His people.

The peace that passes understanding has nothing to

do with circumstances or happenings. It has to do with a relationship to God Himself.

Can we live continually in a state of blessedness? Of course. Jesus says we can.

How is it accomplished? By reading the Word of God and *doing* it. Dabbling won't get the job done. Continual application of principles will always produce results.

Read more about His peace in *King's Kid* 24; *Goo* 62–63; *Victory* 299–300.

Pearls, Victory 205
Peter, Victory 28, 203
Pharaoh, Victory 49–50; God's in Charge 113–14
Philip, Victory 162–65; God's in Charge 97, 113

Philosophy

God's answer: Beware lest any man spoil you through philosophy and vain deceit, after the tradition of men, after the rudiments of the world, and not after Christ. (Colossians 2:8)

And again, The Lord knoweth the thoughts of the wise, that they are vain. Therefore let no man glory in men. For all things are your's. (1 Corinthians 3:20–21)

Wherefore lay apart all filthiness and superfluity of naughtiness, and receive with meekness the engrafted word, which is able to save your souls. But be ye doers of the word, and not hearers only, deceiving your own selves. (James 1:21–22)

Comments and mini-report: Philosophy—or religion—is totally a head trip or exercise of the mind.

The philosopher is never required to prove his beliefs. They are of his own choice and selection and are never exposed to the laboratory of life's trials.

That's why Christianity is not a philosophy or religion but a living relationship with a living God.

Read more about these things in *King's Kid* 167–71; *Victory* 18–23, 293–300.

Pity Parties

God's answer: Casting down imaginations, and every high thing that exalteth itself against the knowledge of God, and bringing into captivity every thought to the obedience of Christ. (2 Corinthians 10:5)

It is the thought-life that pollutes. For from within, out of men's hearts, come evil thoughts of lust, theft, murder, adultery, wanting what belongs to others, wickedness, deceit, lewdness, envy, slander, pride, and all other folly. All these vile things come from within; they are what pollute you and make you unfit for God. (Mark 7:20–23 TLB)

Let the words of my mouth, and the meditation of my heart, be acceptable in thy sight, O Lord, my strength, and my redeemer. (Psalms 19:14)

For as he thinketh in his heart, so is he. (Proverbs 23:7a)

Comments and mini-report: The greatest thief of serenity and peace of mind is self-pity.

"Poor little ole me, nobody understands the cross I bear—sniff, sniff."

That is the attitude of the emotionally sick person desiring to dump the cancerous, smoldering, inner "burned up" condition on someone else's sympathy.

Don't ever fall for it!

The pity party covers up a much more serious attitude—murder!

A strong statement? The Bible bears me out. Check the "pity-party psalm" for yourself (Psalm 137). Have you ever noticed that they were crying their eyes out with being sorry for themselves in the first verse and dashing the babies against the rocks in the last verse? Who can afford the first step of a pity party? Not me!

More about pity parties in *King's Kid* 72, 108, 142, 204; *Winner* 37, 99; *Victory* 73, 106, 160, 197, 305; *Live the Bible* 97–100; *God's in Charge* 61.

Plato, King's Kid 20

Poison

God's answer: And these signs shall follow them that believe . . . and if they drink any deadly thing, it shall not hurt them. (Mark 16:17–18a)

Comments and mini-report: Can God cancel out the fatal effects of self-ingested poison? Can King's kids literally "drink any deadly thing and it will not harm them"? That's what Jesus said, and it must be so.

When the hand of God is on a person's life, and His will for that person is an extended period on planet earth, nothing can destroy that person or thwart God's will for him by premature graduation.

I've heard numerous reports about such things from other people, but more personally, I have experienced them for myself.

For instance? My daughter was on her deathbed from an overdose of deadly chemicals. According to the medical experts, there was no way she could live until morning.

Did we have a funeral? No, because Jesus intervened when we interceded. The miracle took place. Read all about it in *King's Kid* 152–55.

More reports of poisonous doings in *King's Kid* 111–12, 152–55; *Victory* 96.

Poker. See **Gambling**

Possessiveness. See **Ownership vs. Stewardship**

Potter and the Clay

God's answer: But now, O Lord, thou art our father; we are the clay, and thou our potter; and we all are the work of thy hand. (Isaiah 64:8)

O house of Israel, cannot I do with you as this potter? saith the Lord. Behold, as the clay is in the potter's hand, so are ye in mine hand, O house of Israel. (Jeremiah 18:6)

Hath not the potter power over the clay, of the same lump to make one vessel unto honour, and another unto dishonour? (Romans 9:21)

Comments and mini-report: Pottery making was my hobby for many years, and my stoneware and porcelain pieces were quite good. In fact, several gift shops featured them.

Then I met the Master Potter and asked Him to teach me what I needed to know about living the Christian life.

"Refer back to your experiences with pottery making," He directed.

I did, and how simple it all became to just relax in the hands of the Master Potter, whose signature is on the masterpieces of His own making even before we turn into finished products!

Read all about it in *Victory* 53–60. There's more about the Master Potter in *God's in Charge* 137.

Power Hookup, Winner 75–77

Power Shortage

God's answer: But you shall receive power, when the Holy Spirit has come upon you. (Acts 1:8a RSV)

John answered, saying unto them all, I indeed baptize you with water; but one mightier than I cometh, the latchet of whose shoes I am not worthy to unloose: he shall baptize you with the Holy Ghost and with fire. (Luke 3:16)

Behold, I give unto you power to tread on serpents and scorpions, and over all the power of the enemy: and nothing shall by any means hurt you. (Luke 10:19)

But as many as received him, to them gave he power to become the sons of God, even to them that believe on his name. (John 1:12)

That he would grant you, according to the riches of his glory, to be strengthened with might by his Spirit in the inner man. (Ephesians 3:16)

God is my strength and power: and he maketh my way perfect. (2 Samuel 22:33)

Comments and mini-report: As a new Christian, I was eager to share Jesus with my pagan friends, but I soon discovered that I lacked the power to witness.

My pastor told me, "There's nothing to it. Just go

out into the neighborhood and ring a doorbell and pray." I did. I rang a doorbell and prayed—that there would be no one at home. I had nothing to say—and I knew they didn't want to hear it anyhow.

Where was the holy boldness manifested throughout the New Testament? My pastor couldn't help me, but I found out anyhow.

For details, read *King's Kid* 53–58; *Winner* 15–20; *Victory* 84–89, 250–52.

Praise in Adversity (see also **Sacrifice of Praise** and specific adversities, for example, **Arthritis; Firebombs; Heart Trouble; Highway Accidents; Lions,** and so on) *God's answer:* I will bless the Lord at all times: his praise shall continually be in my mouth. (Psalms 34:1)

Whoso offereth praise glorifieth me: and to him that ordereth his conversation aright will I shew the salvation of God. (Psalms 50:23)

But thou art holy, O thou that inhabitest the praises of Israel. (Psalms 22:3)

O praise the Lord, all ye nations: praise him, all ye people. For his merciful kindness is great toward us: and the truth of the Lord endureth for ever. Praise ye the Lord. (Psalms 117:1–2)

Comments and mini-report: The logical mind says it's foolish and hypocritical to praise God when you don't feel like it.

But God says to praise Him regardless of feelings.

Who's right? Look at the results. Expecting to prosper and be in health any way but God's way is asking for second best.

Wrapping up everything in praise and turning it over to Jesus creates the atmosphere where God can work unrestricted to bring about results.

For how it works, see *King's Kid* 125–45, 207–13; *Winner* 39–47, 56–58, 85–93, 95–100, 116–20, 132–33, 169–74; *Victory* 44–46, 68–71, 184–87, 219–21; *Live the Bible* 37–96, 102–25; *God's in Charge* 103.

Prayer, Answered

God's answer: And whatsoever we ask, we receive of him, because we keep his commandments, and do those things that are pleasing in his sight. (1 John 3:22)

And this is the confidence that we have in him, that, if we ask any thing according to his will, he heareth us: And if we know that he hear us, whatsoever we ask, we know that we have the petitions that we desired of him. (1 John 5:14–15)

Therefore I say unto you, What things soever ye desire, when ye pray, believe that ye receive them, and ye shall have them. And when ye stand praying, forgive, if ye have ought against any: that your Father also which is in heaven may forgive you your trespasses. (Mark 11:24–25)

Verily I say unto you, Whatsoever ye shall bind on earth shall be bound in heaven: and whatsoever ye shall loose on earth shall be loosed in heaven. (Matthew 18:18)

If ye abide in me, and my words abide in you, ye shall ask what ye will, and it shall be done unto you. (John 15:7)

Delight thyself also in the Lord; and he shall give thee the desires of thine heart. (Psalms 37:4)

But they that wait upon the Lord shall renew their strength; they shall mount up with wings as eagles; they shall run, and not be weary; and they shall walk, and not faint. (Isaiah 40:31b)

But if any man be a worshipper of God, and doeth his will, him he heareth. (John 9:31)

Comments and mini-report: Does God always answer prayer?

Of course.

Does He always answer in the way we expect?

Praise God, *no!* If He did, we would be in messes of our own choosing most of the time.

What do *we* have to do with prayer answers? A whole lot, if the Bible is true.

There are three basic roadblocks to answered prayer, that is, to receiving direct answers from heaven to specific requests. (For details, consult **Roadblocks** in this index.) Overlooking these hindrances leads to confusion about how God works in our lives.

Some folks ignorantly demand that God act in a certain situation—without taking into account these hidden inner impediments. Then they claim that God no longer answers as He once did. All the time, the fault is within themselves.

Dispensationalism, that great robber of blessings in the lives of King's kids, probably began through neglect of the principles involved in dealing with these hindrances.

Healing of memories can also be an evasion of this principle. Become aware of how things *really* work. You owe it to yourself.

For some cases where prayer was answered, try *Winner* 101–6; *Victory* 70–71, 105–14. And *Live the Bible* is full of that kind of high victory in Jesus.

Prayer Failure (see also **Fullness of Time),** God's in Charge 71–84, 91–101
Prayer for Flabbos, Flab 51–57

Prayer in the Spirit (see also **Tongues)**
God's answer: Wherefore let him that speaketh in an unknown tongue pray that he may interpret. For if I pray in an unknown tongue, my spirit prayeth, but my understanding is unfruitful. What is it then? I will pray with the spirit, and I will pray with the understanding also: I will sing with the spirit, and I will sing with the understanding also. (1 Corinthians 14:13–15)

Praying always with all prayer and supplication in the Spirit, and watching thereunto with all perseverance and supplication for all saints. (Ephesians 6:18)

But ye, beloved, building up yourselves on your most holy faith, praying in the Holy Ghost. (Jude 20)

Comments and mini-report: "For we pray with the understanding and we pray in the Spirit" is the way God says it through Paul.

Without utilizing both of these dimensions of prayer, we miss insights and information necessary to minister to the needs of people to whom we are sent by the Spirit.

Praying in the Spirit is, in effect, getting on the "hot line" to heaven, where the enemy cannot interfere with God's perfect prayer through us. No wiretapping is possible as we pray in our heavenly language direct to the throne of grace.

143

Obedience to God's directive to "pray without ceasing" is something I could never do with my mind. Can you?

For a fantastic example of what the Lord can do when a King's kid prays in the Spirit, read *King's Kid* 121–23.

Prayer, Intercessory

God's answer: Likewise the Spirit also helpeth our infirmities: for we know not what we should pray for as we ought: but the Spirit itself maketh intercession for us with groanings which cannot be uttered. (Romans 8:26)

I exhort therefore, that, first of all, supplications, prayers, intercessions, and giving of thanks, be made for all men. (1 Timothy 2:1)

Confess your faults one to another, and pray one for another, that ye may be healed. (James 5:16a)

Praying always with all prayer and supplication in the Spirit, and watching thereunto with all perseverance and supplication for all saints. (Ephesians 6:18)

Comments and mini-report: The only ministry without hang-ups or ego involvement is that of secret intercessory prayer.

No one knows what you are up to—including the enemy—if you pray in your heavenly language.

People can never change the minds of other people.

144

Only God can do that, and He does when people intercede for one another by praying in the Spirit.

It happens all the time.

For instance? Well, try *King's Kid* 1–7, 79–85, 112–16, 121–22, 152–55; *Winner* 35, 86; *Victory* 147, 209, 243–44, 249, 252; *God's in Charge* 71–84.

Prayer of Unbelief

God's answer: Therefore I say unto you, What things soever ye desire, when ye pray, believe that ye receive them, and ye shall have them. (Mark 11:24)

Beloved, I wish above all things that thou mayest prosper and be in health, even as thy soul prospereth. (3 John 2)

And all things, whatsoever ye shall ask in prayer, believing, ye shall receive. (Matthew 21:22)

Comments and mini-report: "Lord, heal him if it be Thy will" is the standard prayer of unbelief often voiced in churches ignorant of what God's will actually is.

Injecting "if it be Thy will" into a prayer every few seconds simply provides an easy-out alibi in case God fails to answer in the way we want Him to answer.

When we know God's will for us absolutely through the blood covenant ministered to us by His Son, Jesus, we can eliminate this prayer of unbelief. Delivered from doubt, we can grow strong in faith as we act as if His Word is actually true.

Then the prayer comes out mixed with thanksgiving that God's answer is on the way, in line with the promises guaranteed in His Word. That makes prayer a whole new ball game!

Read more about the prayer of unbelief in *King's Kid* 184; *Winner* 30–31; *Victory* 252.

Prayer, Proxy

God's answer: And when Jesus was entered into Capernaum, there came unto him a centurion, beseeching him, And saying, Lord, my servant lieth at home sick of the palsy, grievously tormented. And Jesus saith unto him, I will come and heal him. The centurion answered and said, Lord, I am not worthy that thou shouldest come under my roof: but speak the word only, and my servant shall be healed. . . . And his servant was healed in the selfsame hour. (Matthew 8:5–8, 13b)

Comments and mini-report: I often hear the question "But is it scriptural to pray for someone by proxy?"

At the other extreme, there are those who reason, "If proxy prayer works, why not do it that way all the time?"

Praise God, He is not about to permit us to settle into any specific prayer rut. Just about the time we think we have a doctrinal method for prayer all nicely wrapped up, the Lord takes it all apart again and directs our attention to the "better way" of looking to the Holy Spirit, instead of to a method, to meet all our prayer deficits.

"But what about the faith of the person being prayed for? Isn't that essential to receiving answers?"

When people bring that one up, I remind them that Lazarus had little to offer except decomposition. They usually don't mention it again.

As we prayed for the woman in a mental hospital fifty miles away, did Jesus heal her by proxy? No. He healed her by His presence—both with us and with her. Hallelujah!

That remarkable case is described in *King's Kid* 189–95. More about proxy prayer in *King's Kid* 173–77; *Winner* 155–56.

Prayer, Soaking

God's answer: Pray without ceasing. (1 Thessalonians 5:17)

Comments and mini-report: "Is it okay to pray more than once about something?" people often ask me. I remind them that Paul prayed three times about his trouble; and that Jesus healed one blind man on the installment plan. Read all about it in *God's in Charge* 126–27.

Prayer Without Ceasing

God's answer: Pray without ceasing. (1 Thessalonians 5:17)

Comments and mini-report: When I first saw God's directive in the Scriptures to pray without ceasing, I said, "Lord, I have only a limited mental capacity. While I'm engaged in solving an engineering problem, how can You expect me to be praying without ceasing at the same time? Be reasonable, Lord. I'm only human!"

Then it began to dawn on me that the verse in 1 Thessalonians 5:17 just *might* be referring to a dimension of prayer I knew nothing about.

That's exactly what it turned out to be—praying in the Spirit.

Prayer in the Spirit bypasses the natural mind and tunes in to the mind of God so that His prayers and ours are joined in one accord, assuring that the answer is on its way.

Praying "if it be thy will" goes out the window,

because when we pray in the Spirit we *know* that we're praying according to His will. With that assurance, then, we know that He hears us and that we have the requests we ask of Him. How do I know? The Bible tells me so—in 1 John 5:14–15. It couldn't be plainer.

"For we pray with the understanding and we pray in the Spirit," God says through Paul. Thus both areas of life are involved, and the supernatural becomes natural to the King's kid who is obediently simple and simply obedient!

More about prayer without ceasing in *King's Kid* 79–81; *Winner* 98–100, 159–67.

Preacher, Perfect, King's Kid 142–43

Preaching
God's answer: For the Holy Ghost shall teach you in the same hour what ye ought to say. (Luke 12:12)

Open thy mouth wide, and I will fill it. (Psalms 81:10b)

Faithful is he that calleth you, who also will do it. (1 Thessalonians 5:24)

Comments and mini-report: Early in my Christian life, the Lord put me in close fellowship with that great man of God, Tommy Tyson, who operates a teaching center near Chapel Hill, North Carolina.

At that time, Tommy was traveling a lot as a Methodist evangelist, and it was my privilege to spend several week-long trips in his company.

On many occasions, as I sat in the church waiting to feed on the Word as only Brother Tommy can deliver it, he suddenly turned to me and said, "Brother Hal, I believe Jesus wants *you* in the pulpit for this service."

He didn't ask me—he *told* me!

Then, as I gasped for breath and hung on to the pulpit for support, Tommy would remind me of the words of Jesus made just for such occasions: "For the Holy Ghost shall teach you in the same hour what ye ought to say" (Luke 12:12).

It always worked—and still does!

Praise God for Brother Tommy and his great patience with me.

For an example of that kind of preaching, read *Winner* 135–41.

Pride

God's answer: Pride goeth before destruction, and an haughty spirit before a fall. (Proverbs 16:18)

But the meek shall inherit the earth; and shall delight themselves in the abundance of peace. (Psalms 37:11)

The pride of life, is not of the Father, but is of the world. (1 John 2:16b)

Wherefore he saith, God resisteth the proud, but giveth grace unto the humble. (James 4:6)

Humble yourselves in the sight of the Lord, and he shall lift you up. (James 4:10)

That, according as it is written, He that glorieth, let him glory in the Lord. (1 Corinthians 1:31)

Thus saith the Lord, Let not the wise man glory in his wisdom, neither let the mighty man glory in his might, let not the rich man glory in his riches: But let him that glorieth glory in this, that he understandeth and knoweth me, that I am the Lord which exercise lovingkindness, judgment, and righteousness, in the earth: for in these things I delight, saith the Lord. (Jeremiah 9:23–24)

Comments and mini-report: When wrongly centered, pride becomes self-righteousness, the final stronghold of Slue Foot.

Applying God's antidote—humility—for this subtlest of all sins is the only way to be free from it.

How do I know? I was one of the chief offenders. You might even find some true confessions mixed into these reports on pride: *King's Kid* 105; *Winner* xvi; *Victory* 77–78, 97, 237–39, 274. But the account that really "tells all" can be found in *God's in Charge* 11–48.

Prison. See **Bum Rap**

Programitis

God's answer: For they being ignorant of God's righteousness, and going about to establish their own righteousness, have not submitted themselves unto the righteousness of God. (Romans 10:3)

The Lord's blessing is our greatest wealth. All our work adds nothing to it! (Proverbs 10:22 TLB)

Comments and mini-report: "Once is a habit" explains the human tendency to set up doctrines, dogmas, and programs and thereby "quench the Spirit" in the life of the Christian Church.

Doctrines of men have had a tendency to become exalted above the Word of God all through Church history. For instance, when I was a new Christian, about thirty years ago, my denomination assured me that Bible-time miracles were not for today.

They said God provided miracles in the beginning to help the early church get into operation, but that they were taken away and no longer functioned. "We didn't need miracles any longer—after we got our programs set up," they said confidently.

Praise God, their programs did not supersede God's working in our church in spite of them!

I'm not against programs. They're good in their place—which is somewhere secondary to the operations of the Holy Spirit. Otherwise they become the "letter that killeth" by blocking the Spirit that gives life.

For some reports on programitis, see *Victory* 153, 215.

Promised Land, Goo 72–73; Victory 31–34

Property Problems
God's answer: Rejoice in the Lord alway: and again I say, Rejoice. (Philippians 4:4)

Fear ye not, stand still, and see the salvation of the Lord, which he will shew to you to day. (Exodus 14:13a)

But my God shall supply all your need according to his riches in glory by Christ Jesus. (Philippians 4:19)

Comments and mini-report: Have you ever had trouble either buying or selling property?

Have negotiations bogged down at the crucial moment when all seemed ready for the final signature?

We have all had such experiences.

But I found a way to avoid all the hassle—a more excellent way. What is it? Ask the true Owner of all property, Jesus Christ, to handle all the details as a knowledgeable owner should.

It works. Foolproof.

We needed property for our business—and none was available.

We needed to sell our home and find a new one just suited to our needs.

Our daughter needed a home of certain specifications.

Jesus met all our needs beyond our fondest hopes when we trusted Him who owns all the cattle on a thousand hills. He'll do the same thing for you—if you'll trust Him.

A couple of testimonies on how this works are found in *Winner* 107–12, 159–67.

Prophecy

God's answer: Follow after charity, and desire spiritual gifts, but rather that ye may prophesy. For he that speaketh in an unknown tongue speaketh not unto men, but unto God: for no man understandeth him; howbeit in the spirit he speaketh mysteries. But he that prophesieth speaketh unto men to edification, and exhortation, and comfort. He that speaketh in an unknown tongue edifieth himself; but he that prophesieth edifieth the church. I would that ye all spake with tongues, but rather that ye prophesied: for greater is he that prophesieth than he that speaketh with tongues, except he interpret, that the church may receive edifying. (1 Corinthians 14:1–5)

In the mouth of two or three witnesses shall every word be established. (2 Corinthians 13:1b)

But the natural man receiveth not the things of the Spirit of God: for they are foolishness unto him: neither can he know them, because they are spiritually discerned. (1 Corinthians 2:14)

Wherefore, brethren, covet to prophesy, and forbid not to speak with tongues. (1 Corinthians 14:39)

And though I have the gift of prophecy, and understand all mysteries, and all knowledge; and though I have all faith, so that I could remove mountains, and have not charity, I am nothing. (1 Corinthians 13:2)

Despise not prophesyings. (1 Thessalonians 5:20)

And the spirits of the prophets are subject to the prophets. (1 Corinthians 14:32)

Comments and mini-report: There are many voices these days saying, "Now listen to *me*. I'm the only one with all the *true* answers."

Are those voices right? Who *does* have the answers? Just who *is* the reliable prophet?

There is only one. His name is Jesus, and He will never mislead us.

The Word of God is specific in the area of foretelling the future, which is one aspect of prophecy. "For no man knows the day or the hour," is the way Jesus tells it.

How can we tell true prophetic utterance from the false variety? How can we be sure of holding fast that which is good and letting the rest go on by?

Only by the measures given by the Word of God in the *Manufacturer's Handbook,* the Bible.

Many brethren preach at other brethren through so-called prophetic utterance:

"Thus saith the Lord, I'll send down fire from

heaven and consume all of you dirty old sinners," is the way I've heard it in some meetings.

Is that a word from God?

Check all so-called prophecy with the measuring rod of "edification, and exhortation, and comfort" (1 Corinthians 14:3; in the NIV, "strengthening, encouragement, and comfort") before jumping out the window.

More about prophecy in King's kid reports in *King's Kid* 65, 158, 192; *Winner* 109; *Victory* 253–58.

Proxy prayer. See **Prayer, Proxy**

Pruning

God's answer: I am the true vine, and my Father is the husbandman. Every branch in me that beareth not fruit he taketh away: and every branch that beareth fruit, he purgeth it, that it may bring forth more fruit. (John 15:1–2)

Comments and mini-report: Pruning does not necessarily take away only useless or sinful things. It is also God's method of removing from our lives anything which stands in the way of heaven's best—even the *good* things which fall short of the best.

To see how this worked in a practical way, I applied it to my grapevines once.

For many years, I had raised good crops of grapes, by proper pruning of new growth annually. Growing up in the country as I did, I learned these things as part of my boyhood training.

Then for one experimental year I decided to allow the branches to grow without restriction, to "do their own thing."

At first I thought I had discovered something good—something better than my forebears knew anything about. There was a great profusion of buds and flowers on every vine!

But the fruit? Forget it. As appetizing and taste-tempting as stainless steel ball bearings. And just about as juicy. Even the bees and wasps turned up their noses at it.

The grapes never reached edible maturity but remained green and bitter—like undisciplined King's kids. I learned my lesson. Have you learned yours?

Read all about my noble experiment in *Victory* 131–35. And there's more about pruning in *Victory* 124–26.

Psalm 23, Victory 151–61

Psychiatry

God's answer: Don't look to men for help; their greatest leaders fail. (Psalms 146:3 TLB)

With men it is impossible, but not with God: for with God all things are possible. (Mark 10:27)

Now ye are clean through the word which I have spoken unto you. (John 15:3)

Therefore if any man be in Christ, he is a new creature: old things are passed away; behold, all things are become new. And all things are of God, who hath reconciled us to himself by Jesus Christ, and hath given to us the ministry of reconciliation. (2 Corinthians 5:17–18)

The heart is deceitful above all things, and desperately wicked: who can know it? (Jeremiah 17:9)

Comments and mini-report: Think you need a psychiatrist? Be careful whom you choose!

For a Christian to consult a pagan counselor on any

level is a great mistake. It's bad enough in financial or business affairs, but when it comes to things affecting the three parts of the person—spirit, soul, and body—watch out! It could be fatal!

Even to listen to an unsaved psychiatrist would be like asking me to repair your wristwatch. I might get it taken apart, all right, but putting all those pieces back together in workable order? Forget it!

Find a psychiatrist who knows Jesus—or keep your mouth shut, *except* to introduce him to the Author of eternal life.

You can read about psychiatrists in *King's Kid* 10, 21, 179–87; *Goo* 63; *Winner* 65–66; *Victory* 35–36.

Purpose for Living
God's answer: . . . I chose you to go and bear fruit—fruit that will last. (John 15:16 NIV)

But you are a chosen people . . . that you may declare the praises of him who called you out of darkness into his wonderful light. (1 Peter 2:9 NIV)

Comments and mini-report: Why are we here? Some wag said we are here because the weeds need the carbon dioxide. But the Manufacturer seemed to have something else in mind. You can read all about it in *God's in Charge* 105–19.

Purse-Snatching
God's answer: Surely he shall deliver thee from the snare of the fowler, and from the noisome pestilence. He shall cover thee with his feathers, and under his wings shalt thou trust: his truth shall be thy shield and buckler. (Psalms 91:3–4)

So shall my word be that goeth forth out of my mouth: it shall not return unto me void, but it shall accomplish that which I please, and it shall prosper in the thing whereto I sent it. (Isaiah 55:11)

Comments and mini-report: Criminologists will tell you, "If a person snatches your purse, let go and give it up without a struggle. It may save your life."

No argument. They're right. You'd better follow their advice—if you want to live, and you don't happen to know Jesus.

But what about King's kids? Can they handle such things differently? Do they get special protection?

Of course they do—*if* they expect it!

You mean God really does respect certain persons above others just because they happen to be His chosen children? Ask the sister in the case reported in *Victory* 19–20! She'll give you a hallelujah affirmative!

Quick Mud

God's answer: Save me, O God; for the waters are come in unto my soul. I sink in deep mire, where there is no standing. . . . Deliver me out of the mire, and let me not sink: let me be delivered from them that hate me, and out of the deep waters. (Psalms 69:1–2a, 14)

Comments and mini-report: Falling into a pool of quick mud is generally fatal unless help is fast in coming.

Quick mud consists of tiny particles of material which have no stickiness but act more like tiny ebony golf balls which roll under the body of the victim and tend to suck him down into the bottomless depths. The harder you struggle, the faster you vanish—on a permanent basis.

The day I fell into that pond, I was well aware of the danger involved. Many times I had tossed large rocks into that black ooze and watched them slowly sinking out of sight in a scary, fatal sort of way.

Now there *I* was, slowly disappearing from view forever, with no one in sight to help me, no one in earshot to hear me holler if I'd been sufficiently unterrified to utter a peep.

One panicky thought was worse than the rest: "No one will ever even know what happened to me!"

Did I get out of that hungry black ooze? I'm here. . . .

Read all about it in *King's Kid* 17–22.

Reacting vs. Responding

God's answer: As ye have therefore received Christ Jesus the Lord, so walk ye in him. (Colossians 2:6)

But now ye also put off all these: anger, wrath, malice, blasphemy, filthy communication out of your mouth. Lie not one to another, seeing that ye have put off the old man with his deeds; And have put on the new man, which is renewed in knowledge after the image of him that created him. (Colossians 3:8–10)

Ye have heard that it hath been said, An eye for an eye, and a tooth for a tooth: But I say unto you, That ye resist not evil: but whosoever shall smite thee on thy right cheek, turn to him the other also. And if any man will sue thee at the law, and take away thy coat, let him have thy cloke also. And whosoever shall compel thee to go a mile, go with him twain. Give to him that asketh thee, and from him that would borrow of thee turn not thou away. Ye have heard that it hath been said, Thou shalt love thy neighbour, and hate thine enemy. But I say unto you, Love your enemies, bless them that curse you, do good to them that hate you, and pray for them which despitefully use you, and persecute you; That ye may be the children of your Father which is in heaven: for he maketh his sun to rise on the evil and on the good, and sendeth rain on the just and on the unjust. For if ye love them which love you, what reward have ye? do not even the publicans the same? And if ye salute your brethren only, what do ye more than others? do not even the publicans so? Be ye therefore perfect, even as your Father which is in heaven is perfect. (Matthew 5:38–48)

Comments and mini-report: Life's experiences will always provide opportunities to check our polarity: negative if we react, positive if we respond.

At birth, the human personality is basically negative and remains that way until it is reprogrammed by the Holy Spirit of God when Jesus comes into our hearts and we are born again.

Have you ever seen a newborn baby with an outstretched hand of fellowship? Of course not! On the contrary, babies come into this world with clenched fists, ready to do battle for their rights to dominate everyone in sight.

The first words they learn may be "ma ma," but the second ones are sure to be "no no!"

It takes spiritual rebirth to reverse this tendency toward ministering death into the reverse direction of walking in the light with Jesus.

That's why King's kids need to learn Kingdom living as taught in the Word of God. Otherwise we'll never get better than second best—which is sometimes "down the tube"!

To get your priorities straight in these matters, read *Winner* xvii, 173–74; *Victory* 74, 80, 185; *Flab* 33–34; *God's in Charge* 56–59.

159

Rebellion

God's answer: Anyone willing to be corrected is on the pathway to life. Anyone refusing has lost his chance. (Proverbs 10:17 TLB)

My son, despise not thou the chastening of the Lord, nor faint when thou art rebuked of him: For whom the Lord loveth he chasteneth, and scourgeth every son whom he receiveth. If ye endure chastening, God dealeth with you as with sons; for what son is he whom the father chasteneth not? Now no chastening for the present seemeth to be joyous, but grievous: nevertheless afterward it yieldeth the peaceable fruit of righteousness unto them which are exercised thereby. (Hebrews 12:5b–7, 11)

For rebellion is as the sin of witchcraft. (1 Samuel 15:23a)

Comments and mini-report: Rebellion is a part of human nature that needs to be dealt with in order for King's kids to come within the scope of God's perfect will on every occasion.

Rebellion is compared to witchcraft in the Word of God, so it must be a highly injurious character defect of human nature. It is also a defect of long-standing, having appeared in the Garden of Eden and showing up regularly—without intermission—ever since.

The antidote for rebellion is submission to authority. Ouch! Submission is never easy on the ego—if you happen to have any of *that* left—but it's mighty beneficial in our lives as King's kids in training.

You can read about rebellion in *Goo* 51–60; *Victory* 40–41, 158, 182, 282–83, 292.

Recipe for Healing

God's answer: And these signs shall follow them that believe . . . they shall lay hands on the sick, and they shall recover. (Mark 16:17a, 18b)

Verily, verily, I say unto you, He that believeth on me, the works that I do shall he do also; and greater works than these shall he do; because I go unto my Father. And whatsoever ye shall ask in my name, that will I do, that the Father may be glorified in the Son. (John 14:12–13)

Comments and mini-report: "*Recipe* for healing? Recipe?"

Mrs. Brown, wife of my host for the night, sounded surprised.

"You mean God literally gives us a *récipe* for healing?" she asked again, dumbfounded.

"You could call it that," I said. "And since it seems to be troubling you, let's check it out in the Word." I turned to Mark 16 and pointed to the spot where the recipe for healing was written in plain black and white. There were just four simple ingredients, ready for any believer to apply to her bad back condition brought on by a long-ago automobile accident.

Acknowledging the plainness of the recipe, the woman still had to nitpick a little before trying it on for size. "But what if a bad back is my cross to bear?" she reasoned in good religious style.

I don't recall what I answered to that, but finally her misery overcame her theology and she became willing for her husband, her teenage son, and myself to apply the simple four-ingredient recipe for healing her condition.

What were the necessary ingredients? Look them up in *Victory* 99–103. Who knows? The same method might work for *your* misery, too!

Recipes for Flab Flippers, Flab 111–15
Reducing Programs, Flab 99–100
Reliance. See **Self-Reliance**
Reliance on God's Word. See **Doers of the Word**

Reliance on Other People

God's answer: Don't look to men for help; their greatest leaders fail; for every man must die. His breathing stops, life ends, and in a moment all he planned for himself is ended. But happy is the man who has the God of Jacob as his helper, whose hope is in the Lord his God—the God who made both earth and heaven, the seas and everything in them. He is the God who keeps every promise. (Psalms 146:3–6 TLB)

Therefore let no man glory in men. For all things are your's. (1 Corinthians 3:21)

Be not ye called Rabbi: for one is your Master, even Christ; and all ye are brethren. And call no man your father upon the earth: for one is your Father, which is in heaven. Neither be ye called masters: for one is your Master, even Christ. (Matthew 23:8–10)

The Lord will perfect that which concerneth me. (Psalms 138:8a)

Comments and mini-report: God works through people and the everyday circumstances of our lives. Agreed.

But He also works directly—either in spite of people or on account of them.

Until the Lord took my "King Uzziah" completely out of my life, my Christian growth was at a standstill. I needed to learn that I didn't need any go-between but Jesus.

Read about it in *Victory* 47–50.

Religion, Winner 154

Relinquishment. See **Surrender**

Renewed strength. See **Strength, Renewed**

Rental Car Shortage

God's answer: Delight thyself also in the Lord; and he shall give thee the desires of thine heart. Commit thy way unto the Lord; trust also in him; and he shall bring it to pass. (Psalms 37:4–5)

Don't worry about anything; instead, pray about everything; tell God your needs and don't forget to thank him for his answers. (Philippians 4:6 TLB)

He will always give you all you need from day to day if you will make the Kingdom of God your primary concern. (Luke 12:31 TLB)

Comments and mini-report: "I'm sorry, sir, but you'll have to wait at least two weeks for a rental car. This is our busiest season, and we're completely sold out."

The voice over the phone sounded very positive and very final. There were no rental cars available— no vehicle for me to drive on that beautiful October day in West Germany.

But God had specifically approved of my renting a car! It then became a question of believing my heavenly Father, who never makes mistakes—or of relying on the word of the Hertz rental agent.

The next step? No question about what to do, really. I was to act as if the Word of God was true even though all men be liars. I had book for it in Romans 3:4. So I took His Word for it, acted accordingly, and came up with amazing results.

Read about it in *Winner* 121–25.

Resurrection

God's answer: That if thou shalt confess with thy mouth the Lord Jesus, and shalt believe in thine heart that God hath raised him from the dead, thou shalt be saved. (Romans 10:9)

Therefore if any man be in Christ, he is a new creature: old things are passed away; behold, all things are become new. (2 Corinthians 5:17)

Comments and mini-report: "Why does an intelligent, clean-living, kind and generous person like me need resurrection?" asked a student one day when I was speaking on my favorite subject, science and the Bible.

"Because whether you realize it or not," I told him, "all humans who inhabit spacecraft earth are dead on arrival."

From the day we are born, we begin to die. Admittedly, it takes a few years for the haircut to develop a hole in the middle and then to disappear entirely. Also the teeth stay around for a while, but they, too, soon give way to a spacey grin unless a dentist supplies replacement parts.

Why is all this deterioration happening if we are really alive? The answer is, of course, that we're not really alive until Jesus moves in. We're corpses, and corpses automatically look worse and smell worse with the passing of time.

"You must be born again" is not just a good idea— it's an absolute necessity. We either undergo rebirth or remain corpses going downward at an accelerated rate in all areas of life.

What do *you* choose? For the how-to of the only way that works, see *Goo* 67–69.

Retirement

God's answer: And I will restore to you the years that the locust hath eaten, the cankerworm, and the caterpillar, and the palmerworm, my great army which I sent among you. And ye shall eat in plenty, and be satisfied, and praise the name of the Lord your God, that hath dealt wondrously with you: and my people shall never be ashamed. (Joel 2:25–26)

There remaineth therefore a rest to the people of God. For he that is entered into his rest, he also hath ceased from his own works, as God did from his. (Hebrews 4:9–10)

Comments and mini-report: Sudden termination of many years of business activity can be devastating to the human personality. Being a part of something and suddenly becoming a nobody with a gold retirement watch literally destroys scores of people every day.

I was confronted with the retirement syndrome not too many years ago as I approached my sixty-fifth birthday. What would I do with all my time when I was suddenly placed on the shelf after nearly half a century of constant activity in the worlds of science and engineering?

I knew about atrophy, the second law of thermodynamics, and all that. It didn't sound too good. . . .

Without God and His perfect plan for my life, it wouldn't have been too good. It would, in fact, have been a scary time of life.

But God has put me into a totally new career in my

"old age." I'm younger than I ever was and life is more exciting than I had dreamed possible. That's how it is with King's kids who retire from business and go into full-time service for the King!

Read about it in *Victory* 36–37.

Revenge
God's answer: Do not repay anyone evil for evil. Be careful to do what is right in the eyes of everybody. If it is possible, as far as it depends on you, live at peace with everyone. Do not take revenge, my friends, but leave room for God's wrath, for it is written: "It is mine to avenge; I will repay," says the Lord. (Romans 12:17–19 NIV)

Comments and mini-report: Did I *ever* want to get even! The clod had embarrassed me in front of twelve hundred people. The nerve of him! And all because I was teaching the King's kids something they needed to hear—about the great American drug. Read all about how sweet it was *not* to get revenge in *God's in Charge* 63–70.

Years ago, there was another time when I was so determined to get revenge that I carried a loaded gun in my pocket. You'll find the account of how God saved me from what the world would have called "justifiable homicide" in *God's in Charge* 36.

Roadblocks to Wholeness (see also **Impatience; Unbelief; Unforgiveness**)

God's answer: Therefore I say unto you, What things soever ye desire, when ye pray, believe that ye receive them, and ye shall have them. And when ye stand praying, forgive, if ye have ought against any: that your Father also which is in heaven may forgive you your trespasses. (Mark 11:24–25)

Wait on the Lord: be of good courage, and he shall strengthen thine heart: wait, I say, on the Lord. (Psalms 27:14)

Comments and mini-report: Wholeness and healing are miles apart in some instances. That's why Jesus speaks much more about being made whole than He does about the more limited area of healing.

Healing is often accomplished through self-hypnosis, as in Christian Science and other cults. But wholeness, which has to do with the three-part person—spirit, soul, and body—can come only from Jesus.

Many roadblocks may hinder or block wholeness. They need to be dealt with, or we end up in confusion and eventually decide that God is not really interested in our personal condition.

What are the three major roadblocks to wholeness?

Read all about them in *King's Kid* 107, 111, 199; *Victory* 88, 192, 195.

Sacrifice of Praise

God's answer: By him therefore let us offer the sacrifice of praise to God continually, that is, the fruit of our lips giving thanks to his name. (Hebrews 13:15)

But true praise is a worthy sacrifice; this really honors me. Those who walk my paths will receive salvation from the Lord. (Psalms 50:23 TLB)

Comments and mini-report: "But isn't it hypocrisy to praise God when we don't feel like it?"

Someone generally asks me that at King's kids meetings, and I reply, "No, it isn't hypocrisy. It's obedience to the Word of God that recommends this action so we can put ourselves in a position to receive the heaven's best He has available for us."

When all five of our senses tell us things couldn't be worse, and God says now is the time to offer the sacrifice of praise so He can move in and change things, why don't we try it?

The problem, of course, is that our common sense gets in the way.

"It makes no sense at all," the person in trouble generally retorts to any suggestions that he praise God anyhow. And his trouble naturally remains—and grows and GROWS and GROWS!

Of course it makes no sense to our senses—that's why God has to stress the importance of praise over and over again in His Word.

When I first tried it, following His clear-cut instructions, there was no "sensible" reason for even considering such foolishness, but I did it anyway. The results? Wow!

Read more about the sacrifice of praise in *King's Kid* 118, 211; *Victory* 186–87; *Live the Bible* 65–84; *God's in Charge* 94–95.

Satan (see also Demons)

God's answer: For we wrestle not against flesh and blood, but against principalities, against powers, against the rulers of the darkness of this world, against spiritual wickedness in high places. (Ephesians 6:12)

Be sober, be vigilant; because your adversary the devil, as a roaring lion, walketh about, seeking whom he may devour. (1 Peter 5:8)

Submit yourselves therefore to God. Resist the devil, and he will flee from you. (James 4:7)

Comments and mini-report: King's kids never give the enemy too much attention and of course are never worried about his antics *if* they are walking in the light and wearing the full armor of God.

According to the Bible, quite a batch of angels were booted out of heaven for following the wrong leader. These fallen angels serve Slue Foot today as demons.

"Oh, what a silly idea," Ed jeered. "I just don't believe there are such things as demons—not in the twentieth century!"

After that night when he and I were confronted with a roomful of them, his doubts were long gone. Fortunately, the power of Jesus Christ in our lives makes of no account any tricks the enemy can throw our way—but only if we know how to handle these things.

What Ed and I learned that unforgettable night is reported in *Winner* 175–88. And there's more about Slue Foot and his gruesome entourage in *King's Kid* 57; *Goo* 53; *Victory* 95; *God's in Charge* 82.

Scoffers (see also **Unbelief**)

God's answer: Knowing this first, that there shall come in the last days scoffers, walking after their own lusts. (2 Peter 3:3)

Dear friends, remember what the apostles of our Lord Jesus Christ told you, that in the last times there would come these scoffers whose whole purpose in life is to enjoy themselves in every evil way imaginable. (Jude 17, 18 TLB)

Comments and mini-report: According to the Bible, scoffers and unbelievers have been around for a long time, like forever. But God isn't threatened by them. As a matter of fact, He has ways and means of dealing with them that are far more effective than anything we could come up with.

Oftentimes, God deals with scoffers through signs and wonders accompanying the ministry of King's kids who are operating in the area of the gifts of the Holy Spirit.

The local banker at the businessmen's breakfast meeting was present as a scoffer one morning. "The gifts of the Spirit were finished when the early apostles died off," he religionized.

We didn't argue. King's kids *never* argue about these things. They don't need to, because God is with them to demonstrate His presence and the validity of His gifts as we look to Him to handle everything for us—including local bankers.

That day, the local banker was confronted with a gift of the Holy Spirit in action. It was so impressive, he ended up blubbering all down the front of his expensive custom-tailored vest.

"That has to be God," he sobbed, thoroughly persuaded. He had observed God in action through the gifts of the Spirit.

Read all about that confrontation in *King's Kid* 84–85. And there's more about scoffers in *King's Kid* 74.

Self-Awareness

God's answer: For if a man think himself to be something, when he is nothing, he deceiveth himself. (Galatians 6:3)

Look not every man on his own things, but every man also on the things of others. (Philippians 2:4)

Let him who boasts, boast of the Lord. For it is not the man who commends himself that is accepted, but the man whom the Lord commends. (2 Corinthians 10:17–18 RSV)

This I say therefore, and testify in the Lord, that ye henceforth walk not as other Gentiles walk, in the vanity of their mind. (Ephesians 4:17)

Comments and mini-report: In the beginning of human affairs in the Garden of Eden, there was no such thing as self-awareness. Everything was centered in God, and in awareness of His presence.

How do I know? Adam and Eve were naked but had no self-awareness to cause shame. Self-awareness came in with disobedience.

"And they knew they were naked," the Bible says, so they hid themselves when they heard the voice of God.

171

No member of the animal kingdom has ever acknowledged his self-awareness by declaring his self-importance. No cow has ever been heard to say proudly, "I, sir, am a cow."

Only humans have this cancerous affliction of self-centeredness. We get rid of it only when Jesus Christ comes into our hearts and redeems the whole mess, turning us into King's kids in training who are aware of *Him!*

Read all about it in *Victory* 297.

Self-Reliance (see also **Educated Idiots and the Educated Idiot Box**)

God's answer: So what about these wise men, these scholars, these brilliant debaters of this world's great affairs? God has made them all look foolish, and shown their wisdom to be useless nonsense. For God in his wisdom saw to it that the world would never find God through human brilliance, and then he stepped in and saved all those who believed his message, which the world calls foolish and silly. (1 Corinthians 1:20–21 TLB)

Verily I say unto you, Except ye be converted, and become as little children, ye shall not enter into the kingdom of heaven. (Matthew 18:3)

Not that we are sufficient of ourselves to think any thing as of ourselves; but our sufficiency is of God. (2 Corinthians 3:5)

Trust in the Lord with all thine heart; and lean not unto thine own understanding. (Proverbs 3:5)

Comments and mini-report: "Now ask God to help you run your life," was the advice of other Christians right after I was saved back in 1954.

172

That worked for a while.

"Take God into partnership in your life," someone else told me when I was ready for another step. Partnership worked all right for a while also.

And then I came across the Bible way of living—asking Jesus to run the whole show—living His life through me as a container for Him.

Self-reliance was for the birds. Jesus reliance was—and is—the way to go!

Read more about it in *King's Kid* xi–xii; *Winner* 166–67; *Victory* 34–35, 41–42, 75–76, 168–72, 216–21; *Live the Bible* 45–52.

Self-Rights

God's answer: For none of us liveth to himself, and no man dieth to himself. For whether we live, we live unto the Lord; and whether we die, we die unto the Lord: whether we live therefore, or die, we are the Lord's. (Romans 14:7–8)

But so shall it not be among you: but whosoever will be great among you, shall be your minister: And whosoever of you will be the chiefest, shall be servant of all. (Mark 10:43–44)

Verily, verily, I say unto you. Except a corn of wheat fall into the ground and die, it abideth alone: but if it die, it bringeth forth much fruit. He that loveth his life shall lose it; and he that hateth his life in this world shall keep it unto life eternal. (John 12:24–25)

Blessed are the poor in spirit: for theirs is the kingdom of heaven. (Matthew 5:3)

I am crucified with Christ: nevertheless I live; yet not I, but Christ liveth in me: and the life which I now live in the flesh I live by the faith of the Son of God, who loved me, and gave himself for me. (Galatians 2:20)

Comments and mini-report: "But if I don't stand up for my own rights, who will?" was the logical question of my Educated Idiot Box.

"Just how are you making out, standing up for your own rights, dummy?" an inner prompting seemed to ask.

"Not so hot," I had to admit. Being completely honest, I had to confess that I was making a mess of everything I touched.

Then I got smart and turned over to Jesus all rights to myself—progressively, of course—and the results have been high victory ever since.

Read about self-rights and what to do with them in *Winner* xviii–xix; *Victory* 73, 77–81, 298.

Sheep and the Shepherd, Victory 151–61
Shoemaker, Sam, Victory 206
Sick heads. See **Blown Minds**
Sickness. See name of particular ailment, for example, **Cancer; Heart Trouble,** and so on

Single-mindedness
God's answer: No servant can serve two masters: for either he will hate the one, and love the other; or else he will hold to the one, and despise the other. Ye cannot serve God and mammon. (Luke 16:13)

Ye cannot drink the cup of the Lord, and the cup of devils: ye cannot be partakers of the Lord's table, and of the table of devils. (1 Corinthians 10:21)

A double minded man is unstable in all his ways. (James 1:8)

Draw nigh to God, and he will draw nigh to you. Cleanse your hands, ye sinners; and purify your hearts, ye double minded. (James 4:8)

Comments and mini-report: Divided attention always produces a split image or unclear goals. No wonder the results of double-mindedness are so wavery—up and down—and without consistency.

That's why God warns about the state of uncertainty that is brought about by indecision as to whom we will really trust.

Many years ago I made a decision to follow the Word of God from promise to result by doing the Word and becoming a reporter of what happened.

The result? Seven books of results so far—all of them full of high victory!

More about single-mindedness in *Victory* 202; *Live the Bible* 19.

Slain in the Spirit. See **Fall-Down Syndrome**
Sleeplessness. See **Insomnia**
Slue Foot. See **Satan**

Smoking

God's answer: For ye are bought with a price: therefore glorify God in your body, and in your spirit, which are God's. (1 Corinthians 6:20)

I beseech you therefore, brethren, by the mercies of God, that ye present your bodies a living sacrifice, holy, acceptable unto God, which is your reasonable service. (Romans 12:1)

Know ye not that ye are the temple of God, and that the Spirit of God dwelleth in you? If any man defile the temple of God, him shall God destroy: for the temple of God is holy, which temple ye are. (1 Corinthians 3:16–17)

For a man is a slave to whatever has mastered him. (2 Peter 2:19b NIV)

Comments and mini-report: "If God wanted you to smoke, He would have installed a chimney in the top of your head," the religious churchman told me as I struggled to get rid of three packs of cigarettes a day.

As a baby Christian, I didn't find his condemnation too helpful.

I already knew I was damaging this temple of the Holy Spirit, but I just couldn't quit that habit of forty years' duration.

Then I discovered the Bible way—letting Jesus do the quitting for me. Read all about how it worked for me—and how it can work for you—in *King's Kid* 93–97. For an account of someone who wouldn't try the Bible way and continued to puff his lungs out, read *Winner* 179–83.

Spiritual Experience
God's answer: For if any be a hearer of the word, and not a doer, he is like unto a man beholding his natural

face in a glass: For he beholdeth himself, and goeth his way, and straightway forgetteth what manner of man he was. But whoso looketh into the perfect law of liberty, and continueth therein, he being not a forgetful hearer, but a doer of the work, this man shall be blessed in his deed. (James 1:23–25)

Verily I say unto you, Inasmuch as ye have done it unto one of the least of these my brethren, ye have done it unto me. (Matthew 25:40b)

Comments and mini-report: "But God may not want everyone to have the same type of spiritual experience," argues the natural mind of man.

For once, the natural mind may be right. But unless we have *some* kind of very personal experience with Jesus Christ as living Savior and God, in a very real way, we are not really born again.

You can read about one of my personal experiences in *Victory* 11–17.

Spiritual Food, Flab 27–43
Spiritual warfare. See **Demons; Satan**
Spooky Spirits, Winner 71–77

Standing in the Gap

God's answer: Carry each others burdens, and in this way you will fulfill the law of Christ. If anyone thinks he is something when he is nothing, he deceives himself. (Galatians 6:2–3 NIV)

Comments and mini-report: The day I temporarily stopped praising God, rigor mortis would have set in fast if it hadn't been for a brother who stood in the gap for me and kept the praises ascending heavenward. You can read about my near demise—and brother George's faithfulness to the high calling of Christ—in *Live the Bible* 105–7.

Strength, Renewed

God's answer: They that wait upon the Lord shall renew their strength; they shall mount up with wings as eagles; they shall run, and not be weary; they shall walk, and not faint. (Isaiah 40:31)

He leadeth me beside the still waters. He restoreth my soul. (Psalms 23:2b, 3a)

Therefore if any man be in Christ, he is a new creature: old things are passed away; behold, all things are become new. (2 Corinthians 5:17)

Comments and mini-report: When our strength gives out and exhaustion sets in, there is something needing attention in the conditions of our souls or our bodies.

I frequently returned from speaking engagements completely drained and exhausted from only three or four hours of ministry. Now that I've learned how to rely on His strength instead of my own, things are different! So different that even my wife can see it!

For how the eagle renews *his* strength, see *Victory* 213–15.

Stress (see also **Anxiety**)

God's answer: Commit thy works unto the Lord, and thy thoughts shall be established. (Proverbs 16:3)

Thou wilt keep him in perfect peace, whose mind is stayed on thee: because he trusteth in thee. (Isaiah 26:3)

Peace I leave with you, my peace I give unto you: not as the world giveth, give I unto you. Let not your heart be troubled, neither let it be afraid. (John 14:27)

These things I have spoken unto you, that in me ye might have peace. In the world ye shall have tribulation: but be of good cheer; I have overcome the world. (John 16:33)

That he would grant you, according to the riches of his glory, to be strengthened with might by his Spirit in the inner man. (Ephesians 3:16)

Faithful is he that calleth you, who also will do it. (1 Thessalonians 5:24)

Comments and mini-report: Can we actually live stress-free lives here on planet earth? Is there a way to bypass all inner strain and turmoil?

The Bible says yes! Then it tells how.

I tried the Bible way, and it really works. When I'm living the way God recommends, I never experience anything but inner peace and rest.

Want it? It's yours. How? Read on. . . .

King's kid reports on stress are in *Goo* 62–63, 76–77; *Victory* 83–89, 299–300.

Stumbling Block

God's answer: Let us not therefore judge one another any more: but judge this rather, that no man put a stumblingblock or an occasion to fall in his brother's way. (Romans 14:13)

It is good neither to eat flesh, nor to drink wine, nor any thing whereby thy brother stumbleth, or is offended, or is made weak. (Romans 14:21)

Comments and mini-report: Many things are permissible and even advisable and good in the lives of King's kids. But many other things, if carried out, would be stumbling blocks for others.

For instance, I as a redeemed alcoholic can go into a nightclub to witness for Jesus and have done so on occasion as the Holy Spirit directed. But the baby Christian seeing me go into such a place and being still weak in his faith could attempt to follow me and thereby fall into his old ways.

Similarly, for mature Christians to have anything to do with the occult, to read the daily horoscope, or to be seen in places frequented by the world of darkness—even with good motives—could cause the newcomer in the Kingdom to trip and fall into the trap of the enemy.

There is no safe way to dabble in darkness and still remain in the light and lead others to the light.

Read about stumbling blocks in *Victory* 298.

Submission. See **Husband-Wife Haggles; Rebellion; Surrender**

Success, King's Kid 9–12; Victory 76; Live the Bible 24–25; God's in Charge 20–23

Suffering, God's in Charge 11–161

Sugar, Flab 70–71; God's in Charge 64–70, 94–95

Suicide

God's answer: The thief cometh not, but for to steal, and to kill, and to destroy: I am come that they might have life, and that they might have it more abundantly. (John 10:10)

Come unto me, all ye that labour and are heavy laden, and I will give you rest. Take my yoke upon you, and learn of me; for I am meek and lowly in heart: and ye shall find rest unto your souls. For my yoke is easy, and my burden is light. (Matthew 11:28–30)

Let him have all your worries and cares, for he is always thinking about you and watching everything that concerns you. (1 Peter 5:7 TLB)

Comments and mini-report: The tendency to run away from trouble is built into human nature. Adam hid from God when faced with his own guilt.

Trying to hide from God—from whom nothing can be hidden—is the first step. The next step is trying to hide from self either by denying reality or trying to wipe it out of our awareness by suicide. It's inevitable that when we don't have Jesus Christ in our lives, things will become too much for us to face and suicide will appear more attractive than facing an impossible, irremediable mess.

How do I know? I got to that point in my own life and tried suicide. It was the first time I had ever failed at anything. Then I learned that God had something better in mind.

My conclusion? Life without Jesus simply doesn't work. It wasn't meant to work!

Read how God rescued me and other King's kids from self-destruction in *King's Kid* 11–13, 152–55; *Winner* 44–45; *Victory* 250–52, 296.

Supernatural

God's answer: Even the mystery which hath been hid from ages and from generations, but now is made manifest to his saints: To whom God would make known what is the riches of the glory of this mystery among the Gentiles; which is Christ in you, the hope of glory. (Colossians 1:26–28)

But the natural man receiveth not the things of the Spirit of God: for they are foolishness unto him: neither can he know them, because they are spiritually discerned. (1 Corinthians 2:14)

But to which of the angels said he at any time, Sit on my right hand, until I make thine enemies thy footstool? Are they not all ministering spirits, sent forth to minister for them who shall be heirs of salvation? (Hebrews 1:13–14)

Comments and mini-report: If our lives are being lived only on the level of the natural, we're missing out on heaven's best on our trip on a spacecraft called planet earth.

The life of a King's kid is supposed to be made up of the best of two worlds—here and hereafter.

Is that concept too far out for your think tank?

It lines up with the Bible truth that we're already seated in heavenly places, even while we're serving time here (Ephesians 2:6)!

This life in the supernatural is really exciting. Why not try it for yourself? You can read more about it in *Victory* 86–89, 180.

Surrender (see also **Binding and Loosing; Ownership vs. Stewardship; Self-Reliance; Self-Rights**)

God's answer: I beseech you therefore, brethren, by the mercies of God, that ye present your bodies a living sacrifice, holy, acceptable unto God, which is your reasonable service. (Romans 12:1)

Then said Jesus unto his disciples, If any man will come after me, let him deny himself, and take up his cross and follow me. For whosoever will save his life shall lose it: and whosoever will lose his life for my sake shall find it. (Matthew 16:24–25)

And what agreement hath the temple of God with idols? for ye are the temple of the living God; as God hath said, I will dwell in them, and walk in them; and

I will be their God, and they shall be my people. (2 Corinthians 6:16)

But we have this treasure in earthen vessels, that the excellency of the power may be of God, and not of us. (2 Corinthians 4:7)

Comments and mini-report: "God helps those who help themselves," is an often quoted Scripture which is *not* in my Bible!

The *Manufacturer's Handbook* seems to say instead, loud and clear, "God, *help* them who help themselves without regard for You. They're going to need all the help they can get."

Until I learned the secret of surrender, giving up everything to be a steward instead of an owner, everyday problems kept me beat down physically and emotionally. But after I surrendered, the Word of God came to my rescue like a strong anchor. The overwhelming pressures? Disappeared overnight. It can happen for you, too.

Read more about surrender in *Winner* 13–14; *Victory* 53–60, and become a winner yourself, living in high victory because you've surrendered everything to God.

Sword, Two-Edged, Victory 37–38

Taming the tongue. See **Tongue Trouble**

Technical Difficulties
God's answer: Trust in the Lord with all thine heart; and lean not unto thine own understanding. In all thy ways acknowledge him, and he shall direct thy paths. (Proverbs 3:5–6)

And those whose faith has made them good in God's sight must live by faith, trusting him in everything. (Hebrews 10:38 TLB)

Commit thy works unto the Lord, and thy thoughts shall be established. (Proverbs 16:3)

Comments and mini-report: When all human wisdom and knowledge utterly fail to solve technical problems, can we trust God to help us out?

I had never heard about the possibility of such things until I was confronted with a situation at work where none of the usual answers could solve the difficulty.

"Lord Jesus," I prayed, "Your Word says that with God all things are possible. That must include the present situation. What is it, Lord? What's the trouble with that machinery that won't work?"

The word of knowledge came so plainly, with a solution so clear and unmistakably correct, that even I could not doubt it was God's superior wisdom at work.

The results? You can read about them in *King's Kid* 157–65. For other technical problems where God had all the answers, read *Winner* 32–37, 49–53.

Teeth (see also **Tooth Trouble**), Victory 22
Television. See **Boob-Tube-Itis**

Testimony
God's answer: And they overcame him by the blood of the Lamb, and by the word of their testimony. (Revelation 12:11)

Quietly trust yourself to Christ your Lord and if anybody asks why you believe as you do, be ready to tell him, and do it in a gentle and respectful way. (1 Peter 3:15 TLB)

Comments and mini-report: After I met Jesus and became burdened for my unsaved friends to know Him also, I tried to bring them into the Kingdom by the best-known techniques of salesmanship.

I tried the soft sell, the hard sell, the negative sell—and they all failed, miserably. No one came to know Jesus through my ministry, because I lacked the power to make anything happen. Furthermore, I was ignorant of how God operates in human affairs.

Then the Word of God came to my rescue.

"Ye shall receive power. . . ." I saw that power was the first requirement and I got some of that by meeting Jesus as my Baptizer in the Holy Spirit.

Then came applying that power through God's intended channel, my personal testimony.

My friend got saved—and I nearly collapsed in surprise. It worked!

Read more about the power of your testimony in *King's Kid* 57–63, 130–33; *Winner* 75–77, 186–87.

Thermodynamics, Goo 13–15
Think tanks. See **Ignorance**

Thorn in the Flesh
God's answer: And lest I should be exalted above measure through the abundance of the revelations, there was given to me a thorn in the flesh, the messenger of Satan to buffet me, lest I should be exalted above measure. For this thing I besought the Lord thrice, that it might depart from me. And he said unto me, My grace is sufficient for thee: for my strength is made perfect in weakness. (2 Corinthians 12:7–9a)

Comments and mini-report: Scores of sermons have been preached about Paul's thorn in the flesh, and many theories have been offered about it. Paul himself didn't identify it, except to call it "the messenger of Satan."

What was it?

Was it bad eyesight?

Was Paul seriously ill in the body, as many believe?

Was his problem an ugly mother-in-law, as others have contended?

Considering Paul's extremely active life, I doubted that serious physical infirmity was the explanation. None of the other theories seemed right either. Finally, I asked the Lord to show me what He thought about it.

Amazing! Read all about it in *Victory* 43–44.

Thumb, Squashed, Live the Bible 74–78
Time That Marches On, Winner 85–93

Tithing

God's answer: Give, and it shall be given unto you; good measure, pressed down, and shaken together, and running over, shall men give into your bosom. For with the same measure that ye mete withal it shall be measured to you again. (Luke 6:38)

Bring ye all the tithes into the storehouse, that there may be meat in mine house, and prove me now herewith, saith the Lord of hosts, if I will not open you the windows of heaven, and pour you out a blessing, that there shall not be room enough to receive it. (Malachi 3:10)

Comments and mini-report: Until Jesus redeemed it, my wallet was the tenderest part of my anatomy. Just putting a dollar bill in the collection plate on Sunday morning produced a painful tugging at my gizzard.

"If Jesus came to set the captives free, why doesn't He set me free from my pocketbook?" I reasoned one day as I realized my lack of trust in God for my financial needs.

He must have been eavesdropping, because the next thing I knew, the Word of God was coming through loud and clear: "Begin tithing, Hill."

"Tithing?!?!?!" I probably turned purple with apoplexy. "Be reasonable, Lord! You know I can barely make ends meet using ten-tenths of my paycheck. How can I possibly *survive* on only nine-tenths?"

He didn't answer, and I guessed He wanted me to find out for myself. So I tried tithing. The results? They didn't make any sense at all. With tithing, all my bills were paid up and there was some money left over!

Naturally, I tried double-tithing, then triple-tithing. . . . Wow! The more I gave, the more I got.

To read how it works for me—and it could work for you, too—try *King's Kid* 31–37 and *Victory* 79.

Tongue Trouble (see also **Gossip; Negative Confession**)
God's answer: So also the tongue is a small thing, but what enormous damage it can do. A great forest can be set on fire by one tiny spark. And the tongue is a flame of fire. It is full of wickedness, and poisons every part of the body. And the tongue is set on fire by hell itself, and can turn our whole lives into a blazing flame of destruction and disaster. (James 3:5–6 TLB)

Set a watch, O Lord, before my mouth; keep the door of my lips. (Psalms 141:3)

But as he which hath called you is holy, so be ye holy in all manner of conversation. (1 Peter 1:15)

Comments and mini-report: God's Word has lots to say about "tongue trouble," because the tongue is the most vicious and deadly organ of the human body.

For many years I used my tongue to cut people into thin slivers through sarcasm and harpooning them about their weaknesses.

After I was saved, this tendency persisted, and I became a real menace to the peace and good spirit of the church body.

"I'm sorry. I'll try harder to control my tongue," I told people when they pointed out the unhealthy condition of my tongue.

But the harder I tried, the worse it got. Until I finally gave up my do-it-myself improvement plan and went to Jesus with the problem. What happened? He gave me God's only antidote for a poison tongue.

Read all about it in *Victory* 68–74, 241–42.

Once my poison tongue was brought under control, did it stay that way forever? Sorry to say, it didn't. My tongue, like my mind, has to be constantly renewed by obedience to God's Word or I'm in bad trouble. A pair of instances recorded in *Live the Bible* 97–100 and *God's in Charge* 56–59 may help you avoid the mistakes I made, both of which would have led me into premature corpsehood if the Word of God hadn't come to my rescue.

Tongues (see also **Prayer in the Spirit**)
God's answer: And these signs shall follow them that believe . . . they shall speak with new tongues. (Mark 16:17)

And they were all filled with the Holy Ghost, and began to speak with other tongues, as the Spirit gave them utterance. (Acts 2:4)

He that speaketh in an unknown tongue edifieth himself. (1 Corinthians 14:4a)

Likewise the Spirit also helpeth our infirmities: for we know not what we should pray for as we ought: but the Spirit itself maketh intercession for us with groanings which cannot be uttered. (Romans 8:26)

Wherefore, brethren, covet to prophesy, and forbid not to speak with tongues. (1 Corinthians 14:39)

Comments and mini-report: "But the gift of tongues is not for everybody," some argued.

"You're quite right," the Bible agreed. "The gift of tongues is *not* for everybody. It's only for believers."

"But just why would God choose to operate in such a funny-sounding manner?" the rational mind wants to know.

To which the best answer is, "That's none of your business. That's God's business."

What is the benefit of speaking in tongues?

Read all about it in *King's Kid* 79–87; *Victory* 95–96, 235, 240–49.

Tooth Trouble

God's answer: Be careful for nothing; but in every thing by prayer and supplication with thanksgiving let your requests be made known unto God. (Philippians 4:6)

I will bless the Lord at all times: his praise shall continually be in my mouth. (Psalms 34:1)

Comments and mini-report: Praise God for the skills He gives to all members of the medical profession and especially to those adept in covering up the ravages of time right in your mouth—dentists.

Using modern techniques, these men of science can replace your own grinders by making false ones which pass for the original equipment.

So the man with the capped front tooth had been grateful for his "cover-up" job performed by the local dentist.

But God is not limited by the law of increasing disorder—called in the Bible the Law of Sin and Death—which causes aging of our physical parts. He made them in the first place and on occasion furnishes a complete replacement while we wait!

You mean God can supply new teeth?

Ask the man with the formerly capped molar!

More about it in *Victory* 110–11.

Tornadoes

God's answer: The Lord is nigh unto all them that call upon him, to all that call upon him in truth. He will fulfil the desire of them that fear him: he also will hear their cry, and will save them. (Psalms 145:18–19)

And Jesus looking upon them saith, With men it is impossible, but not with God: for with God all things are possible. (Mark 10:27)

Comments and mini-report: Does God change the weather in answer to the prayers of King's kids?

Can we really control the elements by "taking authority over them" as people did in Bible times?

The answer is, "Of course!"

On one occasion, my trip to Kansas City was bogged down while a blizzard raged, threatening to close the Baltimore Airport, from which I was due to take off within two hours.

"Lord," I prayed, "if You want me to speak in Kansas City tonight, You're going to have to change the weather. It's all the same with me. I'd just as soon stay home as to go. But this trip is Your business, and I leave it all up to You."

When I arrived at the airport a little while later, the man at the ticket counter was shaking his head. I gathered he had been shaking it for some time. "I still can't understand what happened to that blizzard," he said. "It was here—and all of a sudden, it wasn't here!"

If he had asked me, I could have told him that Jesus chased it harmlessly out to sea so a King's kid could go west to brag on Jesus.

Read about another King's kid and the elements in *King's Kid* 116–17.

Traffic

God's answer: Many are the afflictions of the righteous: but the Lord delivereth him out of them all. (Psalms 34:19)

Thou wilt keep him in perfect peace, whose mind is stayed on thee: because he trusteth in thee. (Isaiah 26:3)

Have no anxiety about anything, but in everything by prayer and supplication with thanksgiving let your requests be made known to God. And the peace of God, which passes all understanding, will keep your hearts and your minds in Christ Jesus. (Philippians 4:6–7 RSV)

I will praise the Lord no matter what happens. (Psalms 34:1a TLB)

Comments and mini-report: The most painful part of my workday used to be driving to and from the plant in the midst of all that bumper-to-bumper humanity, each one intent on reaching *his* destination first.

Nobody in his right mind gives an inch under such conditions. Why, if you did, you might lose your place in line and never get back in. That's the old pagan attitude which causes so many ulcers and bent fenders for everybody.

Then I learned about "giving in order to receive" and began applying it to driving in traffic. Amazing things began to happen! And I got home without being exhausted from trying to beat everyone else away from green lights and traffic tie-ups.

Believe it or not, I haven't suffered a wrinkled fender or a knot in the pit of my stomach since I started—and kept on—helping the other person to get ahead of me!

You can read about some of my exciting adventures in traffic in *King's Kid* 89–92; *Winner* 85–93.

Tragedy. See **Bad Things**
Tranquilizers, God's in Charge 82

Transcendental Meditation
God's answer: Now the Spirit speaketh expressly, that in the latter times some shall depart from the faith, giving heed to seducing spirits, and doctrines of devils. (1 Timothy 4:1)

That he would grant you, according to the riches of his glory, to be strengthened with might by his Spirit in the inner man; That Christ may dwell in your hearts by faith; that ye, being rooted and grounded in love, May be able to comprehend with all saints what is the breadth, and length, and depth, and height; And to know the love of Christ, which passeth knowledge, that ye might be filled with all the fulness of God. (Ephesians 3:16–19)

Comments and mini-report: "But I didn't know I was exposing myself to the powers of darkness," wailed the person in the mental hospital. "Why did my Sunday-school teacher recommend TM to me if it's all that bad?"

I couldn't answer her question, of course, but I have encountered numbers of fear-ridden, pill-addicted, emotional wrecks who started down the wrong road by innocently opening their souls to invasion of demon powers through TM.

The enemy has counterfeits for most things of the Kingdom of God, and TM is a cheap takeoff on God's recommendation that we meditate on *His* Word.

Meditation on a mantra opens the soul to the frequency of the mantra, which is never heaven's best, as it has nothing to do with the Word of God but with some chant that offers built-in trouble to the unsuspecting victim. TM is a devilish deviation King's kids can do without!

For further warnings, read *Winner* 183; *Victory* 293–96.

Travel Agents, Winner 151–57

Travel Snags (see also Air Travel Problems; Blizzards; Car Trouble; Fog; Fouled-Up Flight Plans; Highway Accidents; Hitchhiker; Hotel No-Vacancy Signs; Language Barrier; Rental Car Shortage; Traffic)
God's answer: Not that I speak in respect of want: for I have learned, in whatsoever state I am, therewith to be content. (Philippians 4:11)

But my God shall supply all your need according to his riches in glory by Christ Jesus. (Philippians 4:19)

Rejoice in the Lord alway: and again I say, Rejoice. (Philippians 4:4)

And we know that all things work together for good to them that love God, to them who are the called according to his purpose. (Romans 8:28)

Rejoice evermore. Pray without ceasing. In every thing give thanks: for this is the will of God in Christ Jesus concerning you. (1 Thessalonians 5:16–18)

Comments and mini-report: When we are about our heavenly Father's business, we are entitled to special travel arrangements and privileges—if we simply expect them and act accordingly.

This comes as a surprise to many King's kids who have never tried it.

As I travel throughout the land and in many parts of the world, I find it to be true without exception. Jesus is the best travel agent imaginable!

For a few travel adventures, read *King's Kid* 206–9; *Winner* 113–20; *Victory* 118–20; *Live the Bible* 37–52, 59–62, 69–79.

Tribulation. See **Trouble**

Trouble (see also names of specific troubles, for example, **Arthritis; Back Trouble; Car Trouble; Property Problems; Tongue Trouble; Tooth Trouble,** and so on)
God's answer: Though I walk in the midst of trouble, thou wilt revive me: thou shalt stretch forth thine hand against the wrath of mine enemies, and thy right hand shall save me. (Psalms 138:7)

And call upon me in the day of trouble: I will deliver thee, and thou shalt glorify me. (Psalms 50:15)

Blessed be God, even the Father of our Lord Jesus Christ, the Father of mercies, and the God of all comfort; Who comforteth us in all our tribulation, that we may be able to comfort them which are in any trouble, by the comfort wherewith we ourselves are comforted of God. (2 Corinthians 1:3–4)

And not only so, but we glory in tribulations also: knowing that tribulation worketh patience; And patience, experience; and experience, hope. (Romans 5:3–4)

In the world ye shall have tribulation: but be of good cheer; I have overcome the world. (John 16:33b)

Comments and mini-report: When things go wrong, are they really adversities?

Or are they God's special arrangements for something better than we could ever imagine or plan?

For King's kids who know what it's all about, trouble is simply raw material for the glory of God and more blessings for His people.

Don't believe it? Read all about it in *King's Kid* 112–23; *Winner* 108; *Victory* 44–45, 187, 189–91; *Live the Bible* 37–126; *God's in Charge* 11–161.

Trust (see also Doers of the Word)
God's answer: Blessed is that man that maketh the Lord his trust, and respecteth not the proud, nor such as turn aside to lies. (Psalms 40:4)

The man who finds life will find it through trusting God. (Galatians 3:11b TLB)

Commit thy way unto the Lord; trust also in him; and he shall bring it to pass. (Psalms 37:5)

Trust ye in the Lord for ever: for in the Lord Jehovah is everlasting strength. (Isaiah 26:4)

For the Lord says, "Because he loves me, I will rescue him; I will make him great because he trusts in my name. When he calls on me I will answer; I will be with him in trouble, and rescue him and honor him. I will satisfy him with a full life and give him my salvation." (Psalms 91:14–16 TLB)

The fear of man bringeth a snare: but whoso putteth his trust in the Lord shall be safe. (Proverbs 29:25)

As for God, his way is perfect; the word of the Lord is tried: he is a buckler to all them that trust in him. (2 Samuel 22:31)

Comments and mini-report: What's the difference between faith and trust?

"Trust is faith in action," I tell people. That's one definition I like.

Faith is theoretical until it meets adversity. Then it becomes part of the answer as it is transformed into trust through praises to God for His perfect outcome—before it ever happens.

For instance? Read what happened to Daniel in *Victory* 189–91. And there's more about trust in *Victory* 112.

Tumors, Live the Bible 124–25
Twisted vision (TV). See **Boob-Tube-Itis**

Two (Better Than One)

God's answer: Two are better than one; because they have a good reward for their labour. (Ecclesiastes 4:9)

Again I say unto you, That if two of you shall agree on earth as touching any thing that they shall ask, it shall be done for them of my Father which is in heaven. (Matthew 18:19)

Comments and mini-report: God recommends that King's kids go in pairs to witness, taking a prayer partner along whenever possible, someone to agree with us.

Why is this beneficial?

It has to do with a principle in science known as "synchronized parallel resonant circuits."

When two or more are in accord, there is a maximum flow of power without hindrance. Furthermore, "a threefold cord is not easily broken," according to Ecclesiastes 4:12.

In another place, God says that two praying together is ten times more powerful than either one separately (Deuteronomy 32:30).

Jesus sent His disciples two by two, and when King's kids work in pairs today—one witnessing and the other interceding—amazing things happen. Read about some of them in *Victory* 118–20, 176–77.

Tyson, Tommy, Victory 118–20

Ulcers

God's answer: Bless the Lord, O my soul: and all that is within me, bless his holy name. Bless the Lord, O my soul, and forget not all his benefits: Who forgiveth all thine iniquities; who healeth all thy diseases. (Psalms 103:1–3)

Verily I say unto you, Whatsoever ye shall bind on earth shall be bound in heaven: and whatsoever ye shall loose on earth shall be loosed in heaven. (Matthew 18:18)

If the Son therefore shall make you free, ye shall be free indeed. (John 8:36)

Comments and mini-report: According to God's Word, ulcers are caused by the wrong use of the tongue. In Proverbs 18:8, He says it like this: "The words of a talebearer are as wounds, and they go down into the innermost parts of the belly."

That also sounds like colitis, intestinal disorders, and stomach ailments of many varieties.

Medical science agrees that many disorders of our innards come from wrong attitudes. And, of course, our attitudes show up through the tongue more than in any other area of the body.

Does someone "bug" you?

Better forgive him quick, or it could turn into intestinal flu which comes from causes not yet isolated germwise.

Read more about how to stay clear of ulcers in *Victory* 72; *God's in Charge* 56.

Unbelief

God's answer: Take heed, brethren, lest there be in any of you an evil heart of unbelief, in departing from the living God. ... For we which have believed do enter into rest, as he said ... and they to whom it was first preached entered not in because of unbelief. (Hebrews 3:12; 4:3a, 6b)

But the natural man receiveth not the things of the Spirit of God: for they are foolishness unto him: neither can he know them, because they are spiritually discerned. But he that is spiritual judgeth all things, yet he himself is judged of no man. For who hath known the mind of the Lord, that he may instruct him? But we have the mind of Christ. (1 Corinthians 2:14–16)

Unto the pure all things are pure: but unto them that are defiled and unbelieving is nothing pure; but even their mind and conscience is defiled. (Titus 1:15)

But the fearful, and unbelieving, and the abominable, and murderers, and whoremongers, and sorcerers, and idolaters, and all liars, shall have their part in the lake which burneth with fire and brimstone: which is the second death. (Revelation 21:8)

Comments and mini-report: Unbelief is not lack of faith. It is a negative power generated in the human mind which refuses to act upon truth, regardless of evidence or proof.

The attitude of unbelief is, "Please do not confuse me with the facts. My mind is made up."

What is the antidote for unbelief?

Read all about these things in *King's Kid* 167–71; *Goo* 72–75; *Victory* 31–39, 86–89, 113; *Live the Bible* 19–20.

Unemployment

God's answer: Therefore take no thought, saying, What shall we eat? or, What shall we drink? or, Wherewithal shall we be clothed? (For after all these things do the Gentiles seek:) for your heavenly Father knoweth that ye have need of all these things. But seek ye first the kingdom of God, and his righteousness; and all these things shall be added unto you. (Matthew 6:31–33)

But my God shall supply all your need according to his riches in glory by Christ Jesus. (Philippians 4:19)

Comments and mini-report: Did you know that God has a perfect job for each one of His kids?

Many times I have prayed with distraught heads of families who were out of work or in jobs not really suited to their talents. As we prayed and turned it all over to Jesus, things happened.

Coincidence, you say?

Ask George, the highly trained physicist who was overqualified for any existing jobs in his area. In desperation, he turned the whole problem over to Jesus—along with the needs of his wife and five small children.

Can God manufacture jobs especially tailored to suit the qualifications of His people?

Ask George! Or you can read all about it in *Victory* 216–21.

Unforgiveness (see also **Broken Relationships**)
God's answer: Then came Peter to him and said, Lord, how oft shall my brother sin against me, and I forgive him? till seven times? Jesus saith unto him, I say not unto thee, Until seven times: but, Until seventy times seven. (Matthew 18:21–22)

And when ye stand praying, forgive, if ye have ought against any: that your Father also which is in heaven may forgive you your trespasses. But if ye do not forgive, neither will your Father which is in heaven forgive your trespasses. (Mark 11:25–26)

Comments and mini-report: According to modern medical discoveries, the major cause of cancer, arthritis, and many related diseases is that old state of man's heart—unforgiveness.

The Bible has talked about it for centuries.

David related his physical problems—and the corresponding state of his soul—in many of the psalms.

My own arthritis never responded in the least to prayer, anointing with oil, or the exorcism of demons. As a matter of fact, one preacher cast several demons out of my body, but my joints were as stiff as ever.

After trying everything else, to no avail, I finally did the Bible thing. Wow! I was instantly healed of long-standing arthritis of the shoulder which had just about immobilized my entire right arm.

You can read all about that episode of unforgiveness in *King's Kid* 199–204. Further reports on unforgiveness are in *Goo* 75–78; *Victory* 192–204.

Unity

God's answer: This people draweth nigh unto me with their mouth, and honoureth me with their lips; but their heart is far from me. But in vain they do worship me, teaching for doctrines the commandments of men. (Matthew 15:8–9)

Comments and mini-report: One of Satan's most subtle cults is called the Unity School of Christianity.

I became involved in this religion myself years ago when I was seeking answers to the emptiness in my life. That was before I met Jesus, of course.

"There is no such thing as sin," the Unity people told me. "You are a nice person. Simply find and develop the Christ that is already in you.

"Salvation? Oh, dear me, no," they continued. "You don't need that! We are all going to heaven someday. A loving God would not send anyone to any other place."

In one respect, at least, they were right. God doesn't send anyone to hell. People simply end up there by following the wrong leader. Unity, for instance, will lead a person right down the tube if he follows it long enough.

"But that's judging, Mr. Hill!" I hear someone protest.

"Of course it's judging," I admit. King's kids are supposed to judge everything according to the Scriptures, and the Bible is most specific on the subject of sin. It says there is only one antidote for sin—the blood of Jesus Christ.

For further warning about this cult, read *Victory* 295.

Universalism

God's answer: Be not carried about with divers and strange doctrines. (Hebrews 13:9a)

Beware of false prophets, which come to you in sheep's clothing, but inwardly they are ravening wolves. Ye shall know them by their fruits. (Matthew 7:15–16a)

Comments and mini-report: "But a loving God would not send anyone to hell," argue the Universalists, lately masquerading under a new label called Ultimate Reconciliation.

Perhaps the subtlest of all Satan's deceptions, this cult twists the Scriptures so convincingly that only those King's kids who stay soaked in the Word avoid deception.

Some of the great ministers of this age have ended up preaching this doctrine of devils. Many of God's people are being led astray as they listen to the lies of the enemy, which always appeal to human pride.

I made a thorough study of the errors of this cult, and I was amazed at the ease with which I could consider them truth if I were consulting my human reason instead of comparing it with the Word of God, which never contradicts itself.

God says it is His will that none be lost, they point out. Then the Universalists go on to say that God's will is always sovereign.

But as I read it, God has given us free will to go to heaven through Jesus Christ or to choose hell by rejecting Him.

What do you say?

More about Universalists in *Victory* 276–80, 294.

Unpaid loans. See **Debts**

Unworthiness

God's answer: For all have sinned, and come short of the glory of God. (Romans 3:23)

Ye have not chosen me, but I have chosen you, and ordained you, that ye should go and bring forth fruit, and that your fruit should remain. (John 15:16a)

According as he hath chosen us in him before the foundation of the world, that we should be holy and without blame before him in love. (Ephesians 1:4)

Behold, what manner of love the Father hath bestowed upon us, that we should be called the sons of God. (1 John 3:1a)

But of him are ye in Christ Jesus, who of God is made unto us wisdom, and righteousness, and sanctification, and redemption. (1 Corinthians 1:30)

Come now, and let us reason together, saith the Lord: though your sins be as scarlet, they shall be as white as snow; though they be red like crimson, they shall be as wool. (Isaiah 1:18)

Comments and mini-report: Are you waiting to become worthy before letting God use you to lay hands on the sick?

Then you will never go into action, because God never promised to make us worthy.

How do we get that way?

Read up on it in *Goo* 84–86; *Winner* 185–86; *Victory* 167–72, 275.

Waiting on the Lord
God's answer: They that wait upon the Lord shall renew their strength; they shall mount up with wings as eagles; they shall run, and not be weary; and they shall walk, and not faint. (Isaiah 40:31)

Wait on the Lord: be of good courage, and he shall strengthen thine heart: wait, I say, on the Lord. (Psalms 27:14)

Comments and mini-report: There is a human tendency in most of us to size up a situation, rush in, and do what seems best—and end up in an awful mess. After we have fallen flat on our noses, we look up and wail, "Lord, why didn't You bless it?"

"It wasn't My idea in the first place," He tells us gently. "I have a perfect plan you can use to handle the situation. Let Me know when you're beaten far enough down to give up and wait on the Lord. Then I'll let you in on My plan—the only plan that will work."

One day after I had reached the point of utter exhaustion, I waited on the Lord, and He taught me about the habits of a species of eagle programmed by God to go through renewal periodically. The life cycle of that eagle is a perfect illustration of what we can expect to happen when we wait on the Lord.

You can read all about it in *Victory* 213–15.

Warfare, Spiritual. See **Demons; Satan**

Weakness (see also **Strength, Renewed**)
God's answer: I am crucified with Christ: nevertheless I live; yet not I, but Christ liveth in me. (Galatians 2:20a)

But we have this treasure in earthen vessels, that the excellency of the power may be of God, and not of us. (2 Corinthians 4:7)

The Lord is the strength of my life. (Psalms 27:1b)

My grace is sufficient for thee: for my strength is made perfect in weakness. Most gladly therefore will I rather glory in my infirmities, that the power of Christ may rest upon me. Therefore I take pleasure in infirmities, in reproaches, in necessities, in persecutions, in distresses for Christ's sake: for when I am weak, then am I strong. (2 Corinthians 12:9–10)

That he would grant you, according to the riches of his glory, to be strengthened with might by his Spirit in the inner man. (Ephesians 3:16)

He gives power to the tired and worn out, and strength to the weak. (Isaiah 40:29 TLB)

Comments and mini-report: A great paradox of the Christian life is that when we are strong, we remain weak, and when we become weak, then we are strong!

In the beginning of my new creaturehood, I was unaware of this important principle and stayed exhausted. Then I learned the secret! It wasn't *my* strength God wanted!

What did He want?

Read all about it in *Winner* xiv–xv, 193–94; *Victory* 42–46, 75–81.

Weights, Victory 75
Wheelchairs, God's in Charge 99–100, 136
Wholeness. See **Healing; Roadblocks to Wholeness**
Will of God. See **Doing God's Will**
Willpower. See **Drinking Too Much; Smoking**
Wisdom. See **Word of Wisdom**

Witchcraft

God's answer: Regard not them that have familiar spirits, neither seek after wizards, to .be defiled by them. (Leviticus 19:31)

Idolatry, witchcraft, hatred, variance, emulations, wrath, strife, seditions, heresies, Envyings, murders, drunkenness, revellings, and such like: of the which I tell you before, as I have also told you in time past, that they which do such things shall not inherit the kingdom of God. (Galatians 5:20–21)

There shall not be found among you anyone who makes his son or his daughter pass through the fire, one who uses divination, one who practices witchcraft, or one who interprets omens, or a sorcerer, or one who casts a spell, or a medium, or a spiritist, or one who calls up the dead. For whoever does these things is detestable to the Lord. (Deuteronomy 18:10–12 NAS)

Comments and mini-report: Many King's kids are dabbling in the occult in spite of clear warnings from God that those who take part in such things are detestable to the Lord. Contacting the powers of darkness in *any* area opens the soul wide to the invasion of demon powers.

People never see anything wrong with these activities until Satan has them hooked. As for me and my house, we're staying clear of every *appearance* of evil, just as the *Manufacturer's Handbook* commands for best results in King's kid living (1 Thessalonians 5:22).

You can read further warnings in *Winner* 183, 188; *Victory* 298.

Witnessing
God's answer: But ye shall receive power, after that the Holy Ghost is come upon you: and ye shall be witnesses unto me both in Jerusalem and in all Judea, and in Samaria, and unto the uttermost part of the earth. (Acts 1:8)

But sanctify the Lord God in your hearts: and be ready always to give an answer to every man that asketh you a reason of the hope that is in you with meekness and fear. (1 Peter 3:15)

No man can come to me, except the Father which hath sent me draw him. (John 6:44a)

And I, if I be lifted up from the earth, will draw all men unto me. (John 12:32)

Behold, I send you forth as sheep in the midst of wolves: be ye therefore wise as serpents, and harmless as doves. (Matthew 10:16)

And the servant of the Lord must not strive; but be gentle unto all men, apt to teach, patient. (2 Timothy 2:24)

For the Holy Ghost shall teach you in the same hour what ye ought to say. (Luke 12:12)

Comments and mini-report: Sharing Jesus with others is what King's kids are all about. Bringing others into the kingdom through the word of our testimony produces the fruit of a Christian—more Christians.

In the beginning of my Christian life I tried to buttonhole folks and browbeat them with Scriptures into getting saved.

Then I learned a better way—wait for them to ask a question. When that happens they're ready for the answers.

So on that flight from Dallas to Baltimore, I had said, "Lord, if You want me to witness to someone about You, have the person in the seat beside me ask a question."

As we became airborne, I realized there was no one in the seat next to mine.

"Okay, Lord," I said. "Maybe You want me to just ease back and take a nap. That's fine with me."

Then the stewardess came along, noticed the little sign-of-the-fish pin in my lapel, and asked, "What does that mean?"

"Thank You, Jesus," I said under my breath. "Looks as though the nap deal is off for this trip."

To the stewardess I responded, "That means I belong to Jesus."

To my surprise she exclaimed, "Isn't that pretty!"

That started revival on United flight xyz! Read all about it in *Victory* 140–43.

And read more about witnessing in *King's Kid* 45–48, 53–63, 65, 70; *Goo* 83–84; *Winner* 21–26; *Victory* 144–48.

Wives. See **Husband-Wife Haggles**

Womach, Merrill, God's in Charge 98–99, 136

Word of God (see also **Doers of the Word; Manufacturer's Handbook**), Victory 34; Live the Bible 16–30

Word of Knowledge

God's answer: But the person who truly loves God is the one who is open to God's knowledge. (1 Corinthians 8:3 TLB)

For God giveth to a man that is good in his sight wisdom, and knowledge, and joy. (Ecclesiastes 2:26a)

... to another the word of knowledge by the same Spirit. (1 Corinthians 12:8b)

Now we have received, not the spirit of the world, but the spirit which is of God; that we might know the things that are freely given to us of God. (1 Corinthians 2:12)

Comments and mini-report: God always has one more fact available concerning any situation than we can ever arrive at by natural means.

This is where the word of knowledge comes to our

rescue—when God reveals through this gift of the Holy Spirit special information to meet the needs of others or ourselves.

Through this word of knowledge, I have solved scores of technical problems in my business and ministered to the needs of many folks with amazing results!

Read all about it in *King's Kid* 1–4, 107–11, 167–71, 189–95; *Winner* 117–19, 129–32, 178–79; *Victory* 234, 266–68.

Word of Wisdom

God's answer: For to one is given by the Spirit the word of wisdom. (1 Corinthians 12:8a)

If any of you lack wisdom, let him ask of God, that giveth to all men liberally, and upbraideth not; and it shall be given him. (James 1:5)

For the Lord giveth wisdom: out of his mouth cometh knowledge and understanding. (Proverbs 2:6)

But if ye have bitter envying and strife in your hearts, glory not, and lie not against the truth. This wisdom descendeth not from above, but is earthly, sensual, devilish. For where envying and strife is, there is confusion and every evil work. But the wisdom that is from above is first pure, then peaceable, gentle, and easy to be intreated, full of mercy and good fruits, without partiality, and without hypocrisy. (James 3:14–17)

Comments and mini-report: Wisdom is knowing what to do next.

When King Solomon asked God for wisdom in

counseling God's people, he was told, "You have chosen the best gift."

When things seem at a standstill and we seek the Lord through the gift of a word of wisdom, things immediately become clear, and we *know* what to do.

"Here is the way; walk ye in it" becomes reality as we rejoice in the miracles which generally follow.

You can read about some of them in *King's Kid* 157–59, 191, 203; *Winner* xv; *Victory* 231–34, 278.

You can write me. Questions and comments appreciated.

Harold Hill
King's Kids' Korner
P.O. Box 8655
Baltimore, MD 21240